ROBERT H. KNIGHT

A STRONG CONSTITUTION

What Would America Look Like if We Followed the Law?

D. James
Kennedy
MINISTRIES

Fort Lauderdale, FL

A Strong Constitution
What Would America Look Like if We Followed the Law?
By Robert H. Knight

Copyright © 2018 D. James Kennedy Ministries

All rights reserved. Written permission must be secured from the publisher to use or reproduce any part of this book, except for brief quotations in critical reviews or articles.

Unless otherwise indicated, Scripture quotations are taken from The Holy Bible, New King James Version, copyright © 1982 by Thomas Nelson Publishers. Used by permission.

ISBN: 978-1-929626-81-6

Cover and Interior Design: Roark Creative, www.roarkcreative.com

Printed in the United States of America.

Published by:

D. JAMES KENNEDY MINISTRIES

D. James Kennedy Ministries
P.O. Box 11786
Fort Lauderdale, FL 33339
1-800-988-7884
DJKM.org
letters@djkm.org

CONTENTS

Introduction		5
Chapter 1	From Abuse of "Free Expression" Back to Real Free Speech	11
Chapter 2	Restoring Respect for Life	21
Chapter 3	Federalism vs. Federal Control	31
Chapter 4	The Road Back to Natural Marriage	41
Chapter 5	From Civil Wrongs to Civil Rights	51
Chapter 6	From Redistribution to Economic Liberty	63
Chapter 7	Taxation with Representation	73
Chapter 8	Restoring a Constitutional Form of Government	83
Endnotes		89

"We have no Government armed with Power capable of contending with human Passions unbridled by . . . morality and Religion. Avarice, Ambition, Revenge or Gallantry, would break the strongest Cords of our Constitution as a Whale goes through a Net. Our Constitution was made only for a moral and religious People. It is wholly inadequate to the government of any other."[1]

— John Adams

INTRODUCTION

In early January 2018, the Federal Emergency Management Agency overturned a longstanding policy that forbade churches from getting federal disaster relief money. The rule change by the Trump administration affected any houses of worship that were damaged on or after August 23, just before Hurricane Harvey devastated large areas of Texas and especially the Houston area. The news came as welcome relief also to congregations in Florida, Georgia, and South Carolina in the path of Hurricane Irma, and to church communities in Puerto Rico that endured Hurricane Maria.

What might seem to be a neutral stance—that all damaged buildings and businesses in a disaster area could apply for aid financed by U.S. taxpayers—was denounced by atheist groups as a violation of the "separation of church and state" doctrine that has governed church-government relations since a series of Supreme Court rulings beginning in the 1940s.

Federal officials' singling out religious institutions for denial of disaster aid is just one of many consequences from a serious misreading of the First Amendment that has turned it from a bulwark of protection for religion into a battering ram against it. Although wrong-headed rulings by liberal judges have fundamentally transformed many constitutional provisions into their opposite, nowhere has more damage been done than to the venerable First Amendment, which reads:

Congress shall make no law respecting an establishment of religion, or prohibiting the free exercise thereof; or abridging the freedom of speech, or of the press; or the right of the people peaceably to assemble, and to petition the Government for a redress of grievances.

America's Founders, and particularly Thomas Jefferson and James Madison, who championed religious liberty, would be appalled at how those very words have been employed to actively discriminate against religious speech and practice.

In many other arenas, the courts have invented new "rights" not envisioned by the Founders or ignored specific guarantees, even those written in unambiguous language.

America still retains many wonderful traits of freedom and a prosperity that other nations can only imagine. In terms of self-identification, we are largely a "Christian country." But in some areas—particularly in popular culture and family law—abuse of the Constitution by so-called civil liberty groups has resulted in decadence, exploitation, crime, and government dependence. That's because the Founders' worldview grounded in Biblical morality has been supplanted by a secularized, libertine view of human beings as detached individuals rather than as mothers and fathers, brothers and sisters, grandmothers and grandfathers, uncles and aunts, and as members of communities.

> Without a deep understanding of human nature as well as God's plan for the family, morality and human government, it becomes all too easy to arrive at rulings and policy decisions that might sound good on paper but are utterly calamitous in the real world.

Without a deep understanding of human nature as well as God's plan for the family, morality and human government, it becomes all too easy to arrive at rulings and policy decisions that might sound good on paper but are utterly calamitous in the real world. As John Adams noted, without God, a society geared to maximum liberty cannot work because citizens would not be virtuous enough to require minimal supervision. To put it another way, the less the populace embraces personal responsibility, the more bureaucrats, police, prosecutors, and prisons are needed. As societal restraints have loosened in the face of destructive interpretations of the Constitution by liberal courts, government has expanded to fill the void.

> Thanks to the genius of the Framers, however, there is a way back from the destructive trends of recent years.

Thanks to the genius of the Framers, however, there is a way back from the destructive trends of recent years. The Constitution itself is the most articulate voice in any legal matter, with plain wording of timeless standards and enough flexibility for their applicability to modern times. Even with all the depredations of dishonest judges and legal pressure groups, the document has proven very difficult to circumvent completely.

Since people are policy, the short answer to how we can restore America's constitutional freedoms and ordered liberty as designed by the Founders is to elect and appoint leaders and judges who respect the original text and unseat those who do not.

Another way is to amend the Constitution in order to curb reckless misinterpretations, such as the Supreme Court's creation of the "right" to legal abortion in 1973 and the "right" of same-sex "marriage" in 2015.

Another remedy would be to impeach lawless judges, something clearly authorized by the Constitution but rarely exercised.

What Has Been and What If?

This book will look at how America has suffered in many ways from legal lawlessness and what would happen if constitutionalism were restored. What would America be like if the Constitution were actually observed instead of being twisted into a pretzel of illogical legal nonsense?

In Chapter One, we will look at how free speech was corrupted by the concept of free "expression," and how to recover its original meaning.

Chapter Two charts how the Supreme Court misapplied the original concept of marital sanctity to other relationships, leading to legal abortion and euthanasia, and what America would look like if this grave error were corrected.

Chapter Three examines what would happen if federalism were properly understood as a clear separation of powers, which the Founders saw as crucial to restraining the growth of a central government.

Chapter Four will trace the legal errors behind the creation of same-sex "marriage," and look at how the negative effects of this misreading of the Constitution can be minimized and eventually reversed.

Chapter Five looks at the transformation of civil wrongs into civil rights, and how the original concept of equality under the law can be reclaimed.

Chapter Six chronicles the evolution from economic liberty to government overreach and some steps to recover the Founders' vision of fiscal and personal responsibility.

Chapter Seven surveys the growth in taxes and spending, and explains why it violates the principle of representational government.

> We should all pray for revival, and in the meantime, work as if revival were just around the corner, because it just may well be.

Chapter Eight summarizes what Americans will need to do to restore the constitutional republic that the Founders bequeathed to us to "secure the Blessings of Liberty to ourselves and our Posterity."

None of these reforms will be possible without a wide restoration of basic morality that can only come from a people who fear God and will follow His commandments in order to choose life instead of death.

We should all pray for revival, and in the meantime, work as if revival were just around the corner, because it just may well be.

"This is a nation founded in liberty. Our fathers came to this country to establish a nation where people would be free to worship and serve Christ. They gave us liberty and law. . . . However, that liberty has always been endangered by, and has been under increasing assault by those who are not free in Christ. Those who are not free in Christ and have not been given new hearts by Christ are inevitably going to try to shift that liberty into license."[2]

—D. James Kennedy

CHAPTER 1

From Abuse of "Free Expression" Back to Real Free Speech

One of the most pressing reforms needed in America today is a return to the standard of constitutionally protected free speech as envisioned by the founding fathers.

Drafters of the First Amendment meant to ensure that people and the press could air their opinions without interference by government. The guarantee "extends not just to political speech but also to speech about religion, science, morality, social conditions, and daily life, as well as to art and entertainment,"[2] wrote former Attorney General Edwin Meese III in *The Heritage Guide to the Constitution.*

Beginning in the mid-20th Century, a different understanding arose in which protected speech became protected "expression." Some of this was legitimate. As Mr. Meese explains, "The free speech/press guarantee also extends to any conduct *conventionally understood as expressive*— for instance, waving a flag, wearing an armband, or burning a flag."[3]

In 2017, the issue arose at the U.S. Supreme Court when a Christian baker in Colorado who had declined

> Drafters of the First Amendment meant to ensure that people and the press could air their opinions without interference by government.

to bake a cake for a same-sex wedding invoked First Amendment protection from having to use his artistic ability to express something against his values.[4] But the misuse of "expression" or "expressive conduct" has also opened the door to a floodtide of pornography and obscenity in many forms, made exponentially worse by the advent of the internet in the 1990s. The good news is that if current laws against obscenity were actually enforced, it would go a long way toward cleaning up the culture. A look at how we got here will help us get back to a society where ordered liberty prevails.

"Off Stage"

Up until 1957, American law and its courts stood strongly against indecency, pornography and their more virulent forms encompassing obscenity. It was well understood that sexual restraint undergirded civilization itself, and that absent such restraints, chaos would reign.

The word *obscene* derives from the Greek notion that some things are to be "off stage" and not publicly shown. Before the cultural explosions of the 1950s, when *Playboy* magazine began to move pornography into mainstream acceptance, even what is now considered softcore pornography was regarded as obscene and therefore illegal. There were sometimes disagreements about what should be allowed, but the ability and duty of government to suppress indecency was not in question. Liberty was rarely confused with license—the absence of any restraints whatever.

> The word *obscene* derives from the Greek notion that some things are to be "off stage" and not publicly shown.

The Bible is quite clear about avoiding immorality: "*I will set nothing wicked before my eyes; I hate the work of those who fall away; It shall not cling to me.*" (Psalm 101:3)

In Matthew 5:28 (ESV), Jesus warns that, "*Everyone who looks at a woman with lustful intent has already committed adultery with her in his heart.*" Elsewhere, numerous passages in the Old and New

Testaments warn against sexual immorality. There is no question that viewing pornography, paying for sex, or patronizing live sex acts violate this clear command from our Lord.

A United Front

America's Christian and British heritage figured strongly for more than two centuries in the maintenance of common decency.

English common laws against obscenity—rooted in Christian morality—are recorded as far back as 1727, and the great legal statesman William Blackstone in the 1760s wrote that the state could prevent publication of "any writings, pictures, or the like of an immoral or illegal tendency."[5]

In the 1820s, many American states enacted anti-obscenity laws with no qualms about their constitutionality.[6] In 1842, as part of the Tariff Act, Congress forbade importing any obscene materials. In 1865, Congress made it illegal to use the postal service to convey obscenity, and enlarged the prohibition in the Comstock Act in 1873.[7]

In *Regina v. Hicklin* (1868), the first obscenity case to reach the U.S. Supreme Court, the justices borrowed from English Lord Chief Justice Alexander Cockburn the definition of obscenity as the "tendency . . . to deprave and corrupt those whose minds are open to such immoral influences and into whose hands a publication of this sort may fall."[8]

> America's Christian and British heritage figured strongly for more than two centuries in the maintenance of common decency.

The Supreme Court Goes Libertine

In case after case, citing *Hicklin*, courts upheld the right of states and the federal government to suppress obscenity. That is, until *Roth v. United States* in 1957, when the Supreme Court began adopting a pseudo-scientific—not moral—definition of obscenity.[9] In *Roth*, it wasn't the specific descriptions of what is obscene that were the problem; most people would find them spot on. It was the new test of "whether to the average person, applying contemporary community standards, the dominant theme of the material taken as a whole, appeals to prurient interest."

This subjective test (think of the community standards of Hollywood versus those of Alabama) left out mentions of morality and long-understood beliefs about the dangers of corruption. The benchmark became flexible. As communities spiraled into decadence, the definition of what "an average person" would find obscene evolved as well.

"The floodgates were opened, and the restoration of any sanity to standards of decency has become very difficult," wrote political science professor Dr. David Lowenthal in his book *No Liberty for License*. "The good sense of previous generations has been forgotten. . . ."[10]

The Kinsey Effect

There is considerable evidence that the Court relied at least partly on junk science in arriving at its faulty conclusions. In 1948, Indiana University zoologist Alfred C. Kinsey published the first volume of what became known as the Kinsey Reports.

As revealed by Dr. Judith A. Reisman's extensive investigations, Kinsey set out to build a "scientific" rationale for any and all sex acts.[11] A credulous media popularized both the male volume in 1948 and the female report in 1953,[12] as did Playboy founder Hugh Hefner, who cited them heavily in his Playboy Philosophy essays. This was the "serious" literary content that helped him get around anti-pornography laws.

Based on thousands of interviews and methods that have since been unmasked as fraudulent and downright criminal in the case of shocking data involving children, Kinsey's "findings" about Americans' sex lives were used by American Civil Liberties Union (ACLU) attorneys to compile the American Law Institute's Model Penal Code

(MPC) section on sex offenses.¹³

The heavily influential MPC was used as a sentencing guide by the courts and by legislators who cited Kinsey's research in order to relax penalties for sex offenses—even those against children.¹⁴ From 1982 to 2000, there were at least 650 citations to Kinsey in law review articles.¹⁵

In Kinsey's view, sexual morality was a myth propagated by an oppressive Christian faith that he had long ago rejected after his extremely strict Methodist upbringing.¹⁶ His libertine view of sex was echoed by Supreme Court Justice William O. Douglas, who was instrumental in steering the Court toward a slippery slide into moral relativism regarding obscenity.

How Free "Expression" Superseded Free Speech

In 1966, the Earl Warren Court, dominated by liberals, heard several cases that further shielded pornography from government censorship. Led by Justice William O. Douglas, the Court lurched sharply to the Left. "Neither reason nor history warrants exclusion of any particular class of expression from the protection of the First Amendment on nothing more than a judgement [that] it is utterly without merit,"¹⁷ Douglas wrote.

Pornographers, then, should be free to produce hard-core material without even bothering to include a fig leaf of literary content. Douglas even argued, like Kinsey, that pornography was a social good, providing "a substitute—not a stimulus— for anti-social conduct."¹⁸

As for the power of government to censor materials on behalf of common decency, Douglas wrote, "the First Amendment, written in terms that are absolute, deprives the States of any power to pass on the value, the propriety, or the morality of a particular expression."¹⁹

If expression in and of itself is protected regardless of content, it's no wonder that years later, some lower courts would confer First Amendment "expressive" speech protection even on nude dancing in strip clubs before being reversed by the Supreme Court in 1991.

"For seven years after the 1966 cases, the purveyors of lewdness, vulgarity, perversity, and brutality felt they were no longer bound by the law," Dr. Lowenthal wrote. "The assault they launched on the civilized sense of morality, decency, and rationality has had no parallels in history."[20]

Finding a Way Back

In 1973, two cases—*Paris Adult Theatre I v. Slaton*[21] and *Miller v. California*[22]—were heard by a Supreme Court that had become far more conservative than in the Warren days. In these cases, the Court rediscovered its moral voice, and made an attempt to put the obscenity genie back into a legal bottle. In *Miller*, Chief Justice Warren Burger took aim squarely at the libertine views propounded by Douglas and his liberal colleagues:

> "To equate the free and robust exchange of ideas and political debate with commercial exploitation of obscene material demeans the grand conception of the First Amendment and its high purpose in the historic struggle for freedom."[23]

> For years, we have been told that pornography is harmless, but now the research has piled up about the negative effects.

In the *Miller* ruling, a series of very explicit descriptions of obscenity are given, and they are so clear that prosecutors have no excuse for not enforcing anti-obscenity laws. The bad news is 1) the U.S. Justice Department and state and local authorities have largely given up the fight; and 2) that by issuing such a narrow definition of prosecutable obscenity, pornographers have been given carte blanche for everything else. Still, it is a target-rich environment for any prosecutor who wants to enforce the law.

Given the highly publicized cases of sexual harassment that exploded in the last quarter of 2017, there may be an opportunity to connect the dots for people about the harmfulness of pornography and to use proof of harm in prosecutions. For years, we have been told that pornography is harmless, but now the research has piled up about the negative effects. A wealth of studies is available at http://pornharmsresearch.com, operated by the National Center on Sexual Exploitation.

Law enforcement officials confirm that in virtually all cases of sexual assault, the perpetrator was a heavy porn consumer.

"In this age of the #MeToo culture when many are willing to speak out against sexual harassment, we need to look to the root cause of male sexual entitlement," said Patrick Trueman, president & CEO of the National Center on Sexual Exploitation and former chief of the U. S. Department of Justice Child Exploitation and Obscenity Section in Washington, D.C.

> That cause is invariably the consumption of hardcore pornography so influential on men and so widely available today. The distribution of hardcore pornography is prohibited by a variety of federal and state laws, and if the American public wishes to curb the sense of sexual entitlement these laws must be vigorously enforced.[24]

That means shaming the smut sellers and bringing public pressure to bear on district attorneys and other law enforcement officials to resume prosecutions.

Conclusion

What would America look like if the Constitution's free speech protections were enforced as intended?

Well, a lot like America before the 1950s, with communities largely free of indecency, and houses of ill repute limited to sketchy areas at the edge of town, where it once was far riskier for men to indulge their baser instincts. Towns and cities would have no problem barring X-rated establishments and keeping their communities family friendly. The Federal Communications Commission would use its authority, granted by Congress, to enforce decency standards on broadcast media. Congress could amend the Communications Act of 1934 to extend that authority to cable.

We would still have the internet, of course, but perpetrators of the worst forms of obscenity would be exposed and prosecuted. A plethora of court cases, some of which involved telephones or the postal service, have demonstrated that content, not the medium, is the salient factor.

> Any of this takes willpower and faith that God's morality will prevail over the devil, who has for too long run wild, with devastating effect.

Any of this takes willpower and faith that God's morality will prevail over the devil, who has for too long run wild, with devastating effect. We need to press legislators and other leaders to take action to restore decency standards, such as removing pornographic materials from PXs on military bases.

Above all, we need a revival of Christianity to turn the tide, for secular arguments alone are not enough. Hearts must be changed.

> Men, in a word, must necessarily be controlled either by a power within them, or a power without them; either by the word of God, or by the strong arm of man; either by the Bible or by the bayonet.

That was Robert Charles Winthrop's warning in 1849 against the inevitable rise of tyranny in societies that forget God.[25]

The first thing to do is to pray for wisdom, guidance, strength and success. Then we can start rebuilding a nation founded in liberty, not license.

"Deliver those who are drawn toward death, and hold back those stumbling to the slaughter. If you say, 'Surely we did not know this,' does not He who weighs the hearts consider it? He who keeps your soul, does He not know it? And will He not render to each man according to his deeds?"

—Proverbs 24:11-12

CHAPTER 2

Restoring Respect for Life

Until the mid-1960s, America had what might best be described as a culture of life. Steeped in Christian ethics, the citizenry seemed to understand the choice given in Deuteronomy 30:15-16:

> *See, I have set before you today life and good, death and evil, in that I command you today to love the Lord your God, to walk in His ways, and to keep His commandments, His statutes, and His judgments, that you may live and multiply; and the Lord your God will bless you in the land which you go to possess.*

Abortion was illegal. So was euthanasia. Apart from instances of abuse, parents had supreme authority over their children.

Sex was seen as legitimate only in the context of marriage. As the sexual revolution was getting underway, the nation was grappling with only two sex-related diseases—gonorrhea and syphilis. Divorces had not yet reached

> Something happened in the courts in the second half of the 20th Century that sundered the many societal safeguards that had protected the sanctity of human life and the institution of the family.

the dismal figure of failure for up to half of new marriages, and a majority of children were being raised by two-parent, mother and father households.

Smut, prostitution and strip clubs were recognized as societal evils and were sharply limited by the authorities. Although the U.S. Supreme Court had begun issuing rulings that conflicted with economic liberty in many areas, it had left "blue laws" and other safeguards in place.

But something happened in the courts in the second half of the 20th Century that sundered the many societal safeguards that had protected the sanctity of human life and the institution of the family.

A Constitutional Time Bomb

The Constitution of the United States is perhaps the most remarkable and durable political document ever written by the hand of man. But it had some major flaws, of which three stand out.

> The Constitution of the United States is perhaps the most remarkable and durable political document ever written by the hand of man. But it had some major flaws...

The first, the permission of human slavery was not resolved for 70 years until the Civil War, the bloodiest war in U.S. history. Then it took another 100 years to overturn overtly racist laws against a segment of the population—black Americans. In both cases, Christians led the reforms—first, to abolish slavery (abolition) and then the civil rights movement.

Today, under our expanded Constitution, with the 13th and 14th Amendments, plus the passage of the Civil Rights Act of 1964 and the Voting Rights Act of 1965, most people find it almost unimaginable that one person could legally "own" another human being, or deny them basic services based only on skin color or ethnicity, especially in a free, self-governing nation.[1] Sadly, that is still the case in some nations that are communist and

African countries ruled by Sharia law, which also oppresses women and minority religions.

The second major flaw of America's Constitution is its inability to contain an out-of-control judiciary, even though America's founders thought that the courts would be the weakest of the three branches of government. They envisioned the executive (presidency) and the legislative (Congress) balancing each other's power, and the Supreme Court being merely a dispassionate umpire.

Over the years, judicial review and the positive law (based on current values rather than timeless written laws) have created a powerful oligarchy in which the swing vote on the U.S. Supreme Court can change history on a whim, as we have seen in rulings that relentlessly swept aside morally-based state and federal laws.

Which brings us to the third major flaw in the nation's most important legal document, and the one we will examine in this chapter: It leaves out families entirely and elevates the individual to the highest level of legal protection. In so doing, it has become a battering ram against parental rights, the family, marriage and life itself.[2]

Rooted in the Enlightenment, this rejection of the common understanding of the primary status of human beings as members of families—fathers, mothers, brothers, sisters, aunts, uncles, grandparents—has led to a series of rulings by the Supreme Court that have bestowed legal protection on practices that for millennia were outlawed for the good of not only individuals and families, but also of communities.

> As with many advances of evil, the changes came wrapped in pseudo goodness and were sold as extensions of Judeo-Christian morality.

As with many advances of evil, the changes came wrapped in pseudo goodness and were sold as extensions of Judeo-Christian morality.

As part of Western society (Christendom), the United States

reflected a Biblically-based moral order. No one had to explain why it was wrong to kill unborn children, prostitute one's body, or to commit sexual acts that were universally deemed unhealthy, immoral and destructive.

The sexual revolution, which began in earnest in the 1950s, planted seeds that came to full bloom in the 1960s, as all values and institutions came under intense questioning.

The Court Invents a New "Right"

This revolution reached the Supreme Court, where the liberal majority suddenly discovered a brand new "right to privacy" of which the framers and generations of Americans had been miraculously unaware.

In *Griswold v. Connecticut* (1965), the Court struck down a Connecticut law forbidding the sale of contraceptives even to married couples.[3] The Court could have done so on the grounds that it was an anachronistic law that no one observed or enforced, but it chose to break new legal ground. The challenge had been brought by the state director of Planned Parenthood, who may or may not have known how this would unleash an earthquake that would eventually legalize abortion and same-sex "marriage."

In *Griswold*, the Court created a new constitutional "right to privacy," basing it on the sanctity of marriage and grounding it in the unstated "penumbra" of the Bill of Rights.

> We deal with a right of privacy older than the Bill of Rights—older than our political parties, older than our school systems. Marriage is a coming together for better or worse, hopefully enduring, and intimate to the degree of being sacred. It is an association that promotes a way of life, not causes; a harmony in living, not political faiths; a bilateral loyalty, not commercial or social projects. Yet it is an association for as noble a purpose as any involved in our prior decisions.

Ironically, those stirring words in *Griswold* were written by Justice William O. Douglas, the man who would almost singlehandedly demolish protections for marriage and decency and help establish another new right—to abortion. The only clues to Douglas's double-mindedness were his phrasing of marriages being "hopefully enduring" instead of being lifelong, and his personal track record, which included four different marriages.

If the Court had stopped at this, it still "could have filled the gap left by the Founding Fathers by serving as the starting point for a new family-oriented reading of the Constitution," Michael Schwartz writes in *The Supreme Court versus the American Family*. "But that is not how constitutional interpretation developed."[4] Instead, the Court warmed to the idea of creating new, taboo-shattering precedents, and performed perhaps the most consequential bait-and-switch in legal history: They misapplied the moral capital of the "sanctity of marriage" to unmarried relationships.

In 1972, a case rose to the high court that accomplished this. Contraceptive salesman Bill Baird, who went on to run abortion clinics, challenged a Massachusetts law against selling birth control devices to unmarried couples. In *Eisenstadt v. Baird*,[5] the Court, citing the earlier finding in *Griswold* (which was grounded in the unique nature of marriage). "If the right of privacy means anything, it is the right of the individual married or single, to be free from unwarranted government intrusion into matters so fundamentally affecting a person as the decision whether to bear or beget a child," wrote Justice William Brennan.

"The right of privacy was invented as an expression of the sanctity of marriage and rooted in the priority of the family over the state," Schwartz explains. "In *Eisenstadt*, the Court threw that doctrine overboard, and made privacy a purely

> The court misapplied the moral capital of the "sanctity of marriage" to unmarried relationships.

individual right."

The very next year, in *Roe v. Wade*[6] and *Doe v. Bolton*,[7] the Court once again misused the "right of privacy" established on behalf of marriage in order to strike down laws against abortion in all 50 states.

The ruling unleashed unlimited abortion, even right up to the moment of birth and has resulted in the deaths of nearly 60 million unborn children. It also has wounded millions of mothers who were persuaded that they were not really mothers to those children, and therefore it was possible for them to undergo the "procedure" without serious repercussions to themselves.

The radical nature of *Roe* went beyond even the establishment of a "right" to abortion. It represented a legal revolution against the family. "The legalization of abortion represents an extreme form of imbalance in the relation of the individual to the family, permitting one family member to kill another," Schwartz writes, "and that it marks the first instance in our legal history since the Roman Republic that intra-family killing has been tolerated by the public authority."[8]

> The radical nature of *Roe* went beyond even the establishment of a "right" to abortion. It represented a legal revolution against the family.

With the claim of bodily autonomy established by way of a "right to privacy," people began to assert the "right" to kill themselves or assist others to do so. By 2018, a number of states—California, Colorado, Montana, Oregon, Vermont and Washington, plus Washington, D.C., had legalized physician-assisted suicide. Although the rest of the country has not yet bought into the chimera that this was an advance in compassion, the logic reducing human beings to autonomous individuals leads directly to it.

We shall see more in other chapters about where the Court's line of reasoning has taken America, but for now, let's look at ways to restore a constitutional right to life in the face of the Left's legal assault.

The Way Back

In previous generations, before the abortion revolution, the Constitution was understood to provide the legal framework for this statement in the Declaration of Independence:

> We hold these truths to be self-evident, that all men are created equal, that they are endowed by their Creator with certain unalienable Rights, that among these are Life, Liberty and the pursuit of Happiness.—That to secure these rights, Governments are instituted among Men, deriving their just powers from the consent of the governed. . . .

What would America look like if the courts followed the Constitution's original intent, instead of engaging in judicial activism? God willing, if more pro-life justices are appointed to the Supreme Court, we may soon find out. The short answer is that far fewer women would be pressured into abortions since abortion would be illegal; taxpayers would no longer subsidize abortionists, and the church and other community groups would be more likely to step up to provide assistance to mothers with troubled pregnancies. A culture of life would de-commercialize sex and restore it as a sacred gift reserved for married couples.

> What would America look like if the courts followed the Constitution's original intent, instead of engaging in judicial activism?

Over the years, the pro-life movement has chipped away at the court-enforced pro-abortion culture and laws. Between 2011 and 2014, states enacted 231 abortion restrictions, according to the pro-abortion Guttmacher Institute.[9] Some ban late-term abortions and others require women to get an ultrasound. Some states now bar the post-abortion killing of infants that survive abortions, despite fierce opposition from politicians such as Barack Obama, who as a state senate committee chairman, helped kill an Illinois version of the Born Alive Infants Protection Act.[10]

Every January since 1973, when *Roe v. Wade* was issued, the March for Life has attracted hundreds of thousands of people to Washington, D.C. The crowds have become younger and younger, as more and more teenagers and 20-somethings have become pro-life.

> America appears to be rethinking the role of the courts, as well as the reasoning that led to the legalization of abortion.

The number of abortions has been dropping in recent years, from a high in 1990 of between 1.4 million and 1.6 million to just under one million in 2016.[11] That is still a tragically high figure since every abortion is tragic. The number of abortion clinics has declined by nearly half since that peak period to less than 600.[12] At the same time, an estimated 3,000 crisis pregnancy centers have opened. One measure of their success is the rising number of legal attacks on them by pro-abortion forces.[13]

Congress has become more pro-life, with pro-life legislation gaining adherents. At some point, a Right to Life amendment that puts protection of life unambiguously into the Constitution itself may well be possible. In the meantime, Congress needs at least to defund the nation's largest abortion provider, Planned Parenthood, which receives more than half a billion dollars annually in tax dollars.[14]

America appears to be rethinking the role of the courts, as well as the reasoning that led to the legalization of abortion. Perhaps we are on the cusp of a time when a majority will transform America by taking this verse from Deuteronomy 30:19-20a to heart:

> *I call heaven and earth as witnesses today against you, that I have set before you life and death, blessing and cursing; therefore choose life, that both you and your*

descendants may live; that you may love the LORD your God, that you may obey His voice, and that you may cling to Him, for He is your life and the length of your days.

"Render therefore to Caesar the things that are Caesar's, and to God the things that are God's."

—Matthew 22:21

CHAPTER 3

Federalism vs. Federal Control

Except for diehard statists who can imagine no reasonable limit on the size of government, there is a growing consensus that the government, especially in Washington, is too big. Too complicated. Too powerful.

What we have now has not just stretched its constitutional limits, but burst through them like an Abrams tank through linen.

The late writer Joseph Sobran, a student of the Constitution, used to quip sadly, that not to worry, "the Constitution poses no serious threat to our form of government."[1] He meant that we had lost the essence of self-government and the separation of powers within a federal system.

Frank Zappa, the late rock star with an acerbic wit, once was asked what he thought of the federal government. "I think they're trying to take over the country," he said without an ounce of irony.

Like a giant vacuum cleaner on the Potomac River, Washington has sucked up treasure and authority from the rest of the nation and shows no signs of stopping.

> The founders' main concern when writing the Constitution was to thwart the rise of centralized tyranny.

The founders' main concern when

writing the Constitution was to thwart the rise of centralized tyranny. Having won a revolution against the King of England, they did not want to start living under an American version. When some clueless former colonists wanted to crown George Washington as king, the first president refused the honor, saying in effect, there will be no kings where "We the People" reign supreme.

The genius of the Constitution is its division of powers. Congress, the courts, and the presidency have their own realms and duties, as do the federal government and the states. The doctrine of separation of powers, credited to the French statesman Montesquieu, plus the Roman and Greek republics, served the nation well up until the mid-Nineteenth Century. Then, thanks to the Civil War and other factors, the central state began to grow.

> The genius of the Constitution is its division of powers.

The Magnetic Pull of Power to Washington

Government expands during times of war and economic upheaval.

As part of his determination to preserve the union, President Abraham Lincoln vastly expanded federal executive power when the South seceded. He went so far as to imprison newspaper editors and legislators in Maryland who wouldn't support his policies, something you don't read about in school history books.

After passage in 1865 of the 13th Amendment banning slavery, two more amendments quickly followed that cemented the federal government's authority over the states.

The 14th Amendment proclaims that "no state shall make or enforce any law which shall abridge the privileges or immunities of citizens of the United States; nor shall any state deprive any person of life, liberty, or property, without due process of law; nor deny to any person within its jurisdiction the equal protection of the laws."

"The Bill of Rights originally gave American citizens rights only against the federal government," Ken Blackwell and Ken Klukowski wrote in their book *Resurgent*. "You couldn't enforce those rights against the states. The 14th Amendment extended federal rights that are deemed *fundamental rights* to also be rights against the states."[2]

And what are these "fundamental rights?" According to the Supreme Court in 1997, they are "deeply rooted in this Nation's history and tradition . . . such that neither liberty nor justice would exist if they were sacrificed."[3] This is worth remembering when we turn to the topic of restoring legal marriage as God created it.

The 15th Amendment (1870) states that "the right of citizens of the United States to vote shall not be denied or abridged by the United States or by any state on account of race, color, or previous condition of servitude."

These two amendments set a national standard for constitutional rights vis-a-vis the states that remains with us today. Later, we will see how the concept of rights expanded well beyond the original formulation and has become their opposite in some cases.

The Elephant on the Potomac

The size of the federal government remained relatively constant with population growth until the passage in 1913 of the 16th Amendment. That's the one that created the federal income tax. Until then, the central government had been supported by revenues from tariffs and other regulatory taxes. Now, it could grow along with the wealth of the country, and grow it did, with a powerful push from progressives who used the White House as the prime mover in that direction.

"Presidents Theodore Roosevelt and Woodrow Wilson had a fundamentally different vision of the executive branch than their immediate predecessors, and indeed really any prior president going back to at least [Andrew] Jackson," wrote Jay Cost in the Hoover Institution's *Policy Review*.

> They envisioned the presidency as the mediator of the national interest—something quite distinct

from what our Congress-centered Constitution prescribes—and thus saw the occupant of the White House as a ceaseless source of activity: communicating to the public about what the national interest requires, placing pressure on recalcitrant legislators, taking an active lead as head of a national political party, and generally rallying the nation to whatever cause he deems important.[4]

Although Republican President Calvin Coolidge followed Wilson and the Warren Harding administration by advocating less centralization and balanced budgets, the stock market crash on Black Friday, October 29, 1929, signaled the beginning of the Great Depression—and another round of government expansion.

When President Herbert Hoover's policies failed to lift the country out of economic misery, Franklin Roosevelt was swept into office in 1932 with the promise of a "New Deal," and wound up winning four presidential terms. During his tenure, the federal government expanded exponentially, with dozens of new agencies such as the Tennessee Valley Authority and the Civilian Conservation Corps.

World War II ultimately pulled the United States out of the Depression, which was arguably lengthened by Roosevelt's redistributionist policies. But the war further expanded federal power, particularly when the War Department morphed in 1947 into several service branches. In 1949, the defense agencies were brought under the burgeoning Defense Department, whose annual budget has now grown to more than $600 billion. As large as it is, the Pentagon's mission and spending are still within the constitutional framework, which assigns national security to

> ...many more federal domestic agencies and programs have had the effect of creating a super state that goes well beyond its branches' enumerated powers.

the federal government, not the states. But many more federal domestic agencies and programs have had the effect of creating a super state that goes well beyond its branches' enumerated powers.

Exponential Growth

The U.S. Supreme Court initially struck down a number of new federal agencies as unconstitutional expansions of federal power but backed off after President Roosevelt threatened to "pack" the nine-member Court with six more justices. Although the proposed law, the Judicial Procedures Reform Bill of 1937, did not pass, it had the desired effect as the Court began rubber-stamping Roosevelt's many new programs and creating new areas of federal authority.

In 1953, Congress created the Department of Health and Human Services, which grew immensely over the next few decades. The next great leap forward was Lyndon Johnson's Great Society, under which numerous programs and agencies were established in the mid-1960s, including Medicare, Medicaid, the National Endowment for the Arts, Head Start, and many others. Richard Nixon created the Environmental Protection Agency in 1979, and Jimmy Carter launched the federal Department of Education in 1980. In each case, the agencies grew and grew, intruding on the states' power.

Out went the Founder's vision of limited government. In came the idea that the government owed everyone cradle-to-grave security, which had long been a goal of the Socialist Party and other Marxist entities.

There are now literally hundreds of federal agencies, many of them duplicative. Government at all levels consumes trillions of dollars in income taxes, plus more trillions in fees.

In Fiscal Year 2018, "total U.S. government revenue, federal, state, and local, is 'guesstimated' to be $6.66 trillion. Federal revenue is budgeted at $3.65 trillion; state revenue is 'guesstimated' at $1.67 trillion; local revenue is 'guesstimated' at $1.33 trillion."[5]

Despite this enormous inflow, the federal government in 2017 reached more than $20 trillion in debt. This would not have been the case if the government were bound by the powers enumerated in the Constitution.

What Would the Government Look Like if the Constitution's Original Intent Were Followed?

For starters, the federal government would be a lot smaller, concentrating on the few things for which it is uniquely tasked, most prominently national security. In *Federalist 45*, James Madison, the Constitution's principal draftsman, explains that the powers delegated to the federal government are few and defined, and those powers are to be principally exercised upon foreign affairs, such as conducting war, diplomacy and foreign trade.

Article I outlines Congress's powers, which include creating taxes "to pay the Debts and provide for the common Defence and general Welfare of the United States . . ." Congress is also empowered:

> To regulate Commerce with foreign Nations, and among the several States, and with the Indian Tribes; To establish an uniform Rule of Naturalization, and uniform Laws on the subject of Bankruptcies throughout the United States; To coin Money . . . fix the standard of Weights and Measures; To provide for the Punishment of counterfeiting . . . To establish Post Offices and post Roads; . . . securing for limited Times [copyrights and patents] to Authors and Inventors . . . To constitute Tribunals [courts] inferior to the supreme Court; [and] To make all Laws which shall be necessary and proper for carrying into Execution the foregoing Powers, and all other Powers vested by this Constitution in the Government of the United States, or in any Department or Officer thereof.

Article II empowers the president to appoint judges and ambassadors and executive office officials, and directs the president to "take care that the laws be faithfully executed."

Article III establishes the Supreme Court and gives Congress the power to create the lower federal courts.

Finally, Article VI, Clause 2 establishes the Supremacy Clause, in which conflicts between state and federal laws are resolved:

> "This Constitution, and the Laws of the United States which shall be made in Pursuance thereof; and all Treaties made, or which shall be made, under the Authority of the United States, shall be the supreme Law of the Land; and the Judges in every State shall be bound thereby, any Thing in the Constitution or Laws of any State to the Contrary notwithstanding."

At first blush this might indicate that the states have no rights if the feds want to override them. But, the Supremacy Clause only specifies "that certain national acts take priority over any state acts that conflict with national law . . . on the same subject."[6]

This is far more modest than some of the Founders wanted, which was to empower Congress to swoop down and veto any state law that they judged to "be improper."[7]

In *Federalist 45*, Madison passionately defended the sovereignty of the states in their own realms of influence:

> [W]as the precious blood of thousands spilt, and the hard-earned substance of millions lavished, not that the people of America should enjoy peace, liberty, and safety, but that the government of the individual States, that particular municipal establishments, might enjoy a certain extent of power, and be arrayed with certain dignities and attributes of sovereignty?[8]

> The states... are supposed to operate like interdependent republics, not as provinces under an all-powerful central government as in many European countries.

The states, then, are supposed to operate like interdependent republics, not as provinces under an all-powerful central government as in many European countries.

At the Constitutional Convention, the delegates secured enough votes only by promising to enact the Bill of Rights, whose 10 amendments are designed to thwart a central government power monopoly and protect individual and states' rights.

The 9th Amendment states that, "The enumeration in the Constitution, of certain rights, shall not be construed to deny or disparage others retained by the people." The 10th Amendment states, "The powers not delegated to the Unites States by the Constitution nor prohibited by it to the states, are reserved to the states, or to the people."

The Founders thought these two amendments would function as high banks to keep the central government river from surging over its designated level of power. As we have seen, they miscalculated, and we are paying the price in confiscatory taxation and centralization of power in Washington D.C.

Finding a Way Back

It is never too late to begin enforcing the actual text of the Constitution. We need judges and courts that will faithfully abide by the Constitution and take back power ceded to the central government and return it to the states.

While the preamble outlines the broad objectives of the federal government, it does not confer any authority to it at all. The delegation of powers follows in the various articles.

Had the Constitution been followed and not subverted by liberal court rulings that diminished the states' jurisdiction while expanding that of Washington, America would be a more vibrantly self-governing republic. We need legislators who will hold rogue federal judges accountable through the power of budgeting or even through impeachment. Then we could see the following:

- The states would have a far more robust role in American life, with 50 different policy laboratories operating where ideas could be tried and adopted by others if successful.

- Churches would be far more active in aiding the poor and elderly, and this would benefit both recipients and givers, since giving is a blessing. It would make the church at once more relevant and vital.

- People would have more money because the federal government would not be taking so much.

- Finally, power would be dispersed over a broader set of jurisdictions in a system of limited government as envisioned by Thomas Jefferson, who above all feared the rise of a second tyrannical government to replace the king.

The beauty of decentralized government is that when mistakes are made, they are limited in scope. If something works, the other states can copy it. When something as large as the federal government makes an error, however, the impact is enormous, as we will see in subsequent chapters.

"But from the beginning of the creation, God 'made them male and female.' 'For this reason a man shall leave his father and mother and be joined to his wife, and the two shall become one flesh'; so then they are no longer two, but one flesh."

—Mark 10:6-8

CHAPTER 4

The Road Back to Natural Marriage

Since the U.S. Supreme Court ruled on June 26, 2015 that men could "marry" men and women could "marry" women, the absurd formulation of same-sex "marriage" has been treated as law in all 50 states. We did not put quote marks around the words "marry" and "marriage" casually. They convey our flat refusal to accept the Court's bizarre reordering of the most fundamental of all human institutions.

Just as the *Roe v. Wade* ruling in 1973 swept aside all state laws regarding abortion, the Court's unconstitutional ruling in *Obergefell v. Hodges* had the effect of nullifying all state marriage laws. Along with more than a dozen laws enacted by legislatures defining marriage as the union of one man and one woman, the Court struck down constitutional marriage amendments approved by popular vote in 31 states, some of which garnered more than 80 percent of votes cast.

Five people in black robes took it upon themselves to ignore all that. They rejected the teaching of not only America's founding religion of Christianity but every other major religion.

> Five people in black robes took it upon themselves to reject the teaching of not only America's founding religion of Christianity but every other major religion.

41

> All judges and justices take an oath to uphold the Unites States Constitution, which rests on the premise in the Declaration of Independence that legitimate authority comes only from laws that comport with "nature and nature's God."

Two of the justices, Ruth Bader Ginsburg and Sonia Sotomayor, had actually officiated at same-sex "weddings" prior to the vote, yet they refused to recuse themselves. That stunning conflict of interest alone makes the ruling legally questionable.

But even that judicial misconduct pales against the reality that the ruling is a monumental rejection of self-government, common sense, biology, American heritage, and the express will of God as made clear in the Scriptures. In all of his usurpations, King George III never did anything remotely this radical, and Americans went to war with him.

While the number of people in marriage units has varied according to different cultures, such as Islam, which permits up to four wives per man, marriage has always been the union of male and female, and in Western civilization since Biblical times, one man and one woman. Same-sex "marriage," then, is an entirely manufactured entity of a denatured culture shorn of its moral heritage. It has no grounding in America's "fundamental rights," which are "deeply rooted in this Nation's history and tradition."[1]

The "Laws of Nature and Nature's God"

All judges and justices take an oath to uphold the Unites States Constitution, which rests on the premise in the Declaration of Independence that legitimate authority comes only from laws that comport with "nature and nature's God." And what are these "laws of nature?" According to the great English legal scholar Sir William Blackstone:

These are the eternal, immutable laws of good and evil, to which the Creator Himself in all His dispensations conforms; and which He has enabled human reason to discover, so far as they are necessary for the conduct of human actions.[2]

Blackstone (1723-1780) wrote that English Common Law, from which America's founders drew the principles of American law, originates in the Bible. God, he wrote, gave us:

> The doctrines . . . delivered [by an immediate and direct revelation] we call the revealed or divine law, and they are to be found only in the Holy Scriptures. . . . Upon these two foundations, the law of nature and the law of revelation, depend all human laws; that is to say; no human laws should be suffered to contradict these.

America's founders referenced Blackstone more than any other English or American legal authority. "Blackstone's great work, Commentaries on the Laws of England, was basic to the U. S. Constitution."[3]

So, if a law contradicts God's law, it is no law at all. Except for a few states that passed laws legalizing same-sex "marriage," the Court's ruling is just that—only a ruling. In either case, it is illegitimate, since it violates the laws of Nature and Nature's God.

> Sooner or later, it will dawn on people that this is not a mere tinkering with a timeless institution but a ruthless attack on the moral order, the rule of law, and America's ordered liberty.

Sooner or later, it will dawn on people that this is not a mere tinkering with a timeless institution but a ruthless attack on the moral order, the rule of law, and America's ordered liberty. Just as *Roe v. Wade* will someday be overturned by a Supreme Court that returns to the original meaning of the Constitution, the *Obergefell* ruling will be similarly dispatched.

If not, we are in for a period of persecution unprecedented in American history. We are already seeing evidence that dissent from acceptance of faux marriage will be punished.

Defending Our Values Is No Piece of Cake

Even before the Court made its ruling, "human rights" authorities in several states began bringing charges against Christian photographers, bakers, florists and wedding venue owners for refusing to help facilitate same-sex ceremonies.

In December 2017, the Supreme Court heard arguments in one of those cases, *Masterpiece Cakeshop v. Colorado Civil Rights Commission*.[4] The ruling, expected in June 2018, could either advance religious liberty and freedom of speech or sharply curtail it. At stake is whether the government can force Americans to express opinions with which they disagree.

> At stake is whether the government can force Americans to express opinions with which they disagree.

Thomas Jefferson would undoubtedly be siding with the baker right now, since he wrote that forcing someone to contribute monies (or in the baker's case, his talents) to advance views that he opposes is "sinful and tyrannical."[5]

Jack Phillips, a self-avowed Christian who owns a bakeshop in Lakewood, Colorado, declined to create a cake for a same-sex wedding. He was charged with discrimination. In his defense, his attorneys argued that Mr. Phillips considers his vocation an expressive art and therefore does not want to be forced to use his art to promote a view that God and the Bible say is wrong. Instead of arguing over religious liberty per se, the legal team emphasized freedom of expressive speech, something that court liberals might actually appreciate.

Helen Alvare, professor of law at Antonin Scalia School of Law at George Mason University, explains this approach:

> *Obergefell* fully embraced the notion of marriage as an intrinsically expressive status, adding that same-sex marriage conveys additional meanings. Justice Anthony Kennedy's opinion affirmed that marriage is understood as a privileged place for intimate association, is associated with the right to bring up children, and is the 'keystone of the social order' as well as the 'foundation of government.' He added that marriage 'embodies the highest ideals of love, fidelity, devotion, sacrifice and family' and is thus the favored 'status for over a thousand provisions of federal law,' which offer 'symbolic recognition and material benefits to protect and nourish the union.'[6]

The "expressive" nature of marriage may well save the day. As Professor Alvare notes, the activists who brought the case are in a trap of their own making.

> [S]ame-sex couples must repudiate this entire line of argument and insist instead that a same-sex marriage ceremony and marriage have no expressive function whatsoever. The Supreme Court should not permit them to have their cake and eat it too.

How We Got Here So Fast

In 1993, Hawaii's Supreme Court, citing numerous now-questionable studies, ruled that the state's marriage law violated the state constitution's equal protection provision regarding "sex."[7]

The monumental battle over marriage quickly spread to the mainland, as Congress enacted the Defense of Marriage Act in 1996. Hawaiians rallied to defend marriage, and later passed a constitutional amendment in 1998 designating the legislature as the only authority that could define marriage law, which they then did. Alaska followed with its own constitutional amendment. Forty-five states strengthened their marriage laws or passed constitutional amendments defining marriage as only the union of one man and one woman.

Homosexual activists responded with a piecemeal strategy of persuading corporations, agencies, and legislators to designate some marital benefits for same-sex couples. Domestic partner policies began turning up in cities, states, and even in federal agencies, especially during the Clinton Administration.

At the U.S. Supreme Court, two key rulings virtually dismantled the legal protections against the demolishing of society's sexual mores. In 1996, in *Romer v. Evans*,[8] the court overturned Colorado's Amendment Two by popular vote, which established a state law barring "sexual orientation" from being equivalent to race in civil rights statutes.[9] In *Lawrence v. Texas*[10] (2003), the court went further, striking down a Texas sodomy law and virtually declaring sodomy to be a constitutional "right."

Majority opinion writer Justice Anthony Kennedy cited findings from international courts and the United Nations as part of the justification for overturning a law put in place by Texas legislators. In his dissent, Justice Antonin Scalia accused his colleagues of "taking sides in the culture war," and of reflecting an "anti-anti-homosexual" bias found throughout the nation's law schools.

> Domestic partner policies began turning up in cities, states, and even in federal agencies, especially during the Clinton Administration.

By 2010, judges were tossing aside laws involving homosexuality using the flimsiest logic since the

Earl Warren Court of the 1960s. In Massachusetts on July 9, 2010, federal District Judge Joseph Tauro struck down the federal Defense of Marriage Act, which had been enacted with overwhelming votes in the House and Senate in 1996 and signed (albeit with little fanfare) by Bill Clinton. On August 4, 2010, U.S. District Judge Vaughn Walker struck down California's Proposition 8 marriage amendment to the California Constitution. On Sept. 9, U.S. District Judge Virginia Phillips struck down the military ban on homosexuality that Congress had passed overwhelmingly in 1993.

The pattern was clear: liberal courts would impose same-sex "marriage" and the homosexual political agenda on America, regardless of what Americans thought. By 2015, all but a handful of states had legal same-sex "marriage," due overwhelmingly to court rulings that struck down marriage laws. Only in four states—Maine, Maryland, Minnesota and Washington—did voters themselves change the definition. A relentless media campaign accompanied the legal revolution, including lots of polls showing that a majority of Americans were wholeheartedly backing brideless or groomless weddings.

The Road Ahead

So how do we get back to a natural marriage-based social culture?

What we need now, as with other pressing issues, is more Bible-believing Christians of all denominations who will confidently expound biblical values regarding marriage in public forums, including entertainment and media. We have to be willing to say out loud that the law is wrong and even oppressive.

Christians also have to take marriage more seriously within the church. We need more marriage conferences and more words from the pulpit about marriage's importance to God and to our own wellbeing. Marriage has already been weakened by casual attitudes toward divorce and "living together," which set the stage for the attack on natural marriage.

In the public square, we need more Christians to register and vote, and to vote their values.

A determined minority, as we have seen with the tiny portion of the population that identifies as homosexual, can effect enormous social change. Of course, those activists have had the enormous advantage of a ruling elite's complicit media, educational establishment, entertainment world, and even much of corporate America.

> ... truth is powerful, which is why the forces of darkness are working so hard to stamp it out. As long as we refuse to remain silent, they cannot win in the end.

But truth is powerful, which is why the forces of darkness are working so hard to stamp it out. As long as we refuse to remain silent, they cannot win in the end. Ultimately, of course, we have it on good Authority that we win, but in the meantime, America is worth fighting for.

On a purely practical level, we need to elect leaders who will restore natural marriage to its privileged place in the law, and see that judges are appointed who will apply the Constitution as written instead of using it as legal silly putty. Even a few righteous leaders can have enormous influence.

We must come to the defense of marriage defenders on campus, whether they are students or professors, who will not bend their knee to the current assortment of politically correct Baals.

We must never forget that we have on our side God Almighty, whose moral laws are timeless and irrevocable.

"Before the state, before the Church, God created the oldest institution on this planet—the institution of marriage," said Dr. D. James Kennedy in a sermon.

It is the oldest and the most universal of all of God's institutions. Wherever you go in this world today, whatever continent, whatever nation, you will find that men and women are joined together in the bonds of matrimony and are rearing families.[11]

"We hold these truths to be self-evident; that all Men are created equal, that they are endowed by their Creator with certain unalienable Rights; that among these are life, liberty and the pursuit of happiness – that to secure these rights, Governments are instituted among Men."

— Declaration of Independence,
July 4, 1776

CHAPTER 5

From Civil Wrongs to Civil Rights

The concept of civil rights has changed markedly in the last few decades following the successes of the black civil rights movement. Led by Christian ministers, most famously the Rev. Martin Luther King, Jr., the movement forced Americans to come to grips with their mistreatment of black people even after the Civil War—and to redress it in the law.

But in recent years, the moral capital of the civil rights movement has been hijacked to unsuitable causes, most prominently the sexual revolution against Biblical sexual morality.

Civil rights have become, in large effect, civil wrongs, in which right behavior is being punished and wrong behavior is rewarded. It is not hyperbole to say that the whole concept of what constitutes a civil right has been corrupted.

By defining Biblical morality as a form of bigotry and then deploying the full government/social/cultural "civil rights" apparatus against it, the progressive Left is very close to criminalizing Christianity in this once-most Christian of nations.

Genuine civil rights are based

> In recent years, the moral capital of the civil rights movement has been hijacked to unsuitable causes...

> "Sexual orientation" is a radical challenge to the core beliefs of all major religious faiths and even to the very notion that sex has a moral dimension.

on protections listed in the First Amendment (such as religion) or on immutable characteristics such as race, ethnicity, place of origin, or sex. When civil rights are accorded to groups defined by behavior that is volitional and has moral implications, the very concept has morphed into something else. What began as a redress for black people following slavery and then Jim Crow has been transformed into a battering ram against traditional morality, complete with legal penalties and open discrimination.

The Trojan Horse that led to this was the concept of "sexual orientation," a made-up term designed to reduce in the public mind the volitional aspect of sexual behavior. "Sexual orientation" is a radical challenge to the core beliefs of all major religious faiths and even to the very notion that sex has a moral dimension. While other activities such as buying and selling remain subject to moral judgments, the concept of "sexual orientation" places sex outside morality. No other human behavior with such sweeping consequences has received such a stamp of neutrality.

The idea is to make it seem as if homosexuality is something people are born with—like skin color. Despite well-publicized—now debunked—studies purporting to show a genetic, and therefore unchangeable, component to homosexuality,[1] the science is not there. Increasing numbers of people who once identified as "gay" are coming out of the lifestyle and even marrying and having children. Because of media bias, they are the best kept secret of the culture wars.

The "born that way" argument to pave the way for civil rights claims has been accompanied by the notion that homosexuals have suffered just the way blacks have in America. With the exception of some truly deplorable treatment of some individuals, which is un-Christian and unacceptable, this is preposterous.

In defining what is a "suspect class," that is, one that qualifies for special protections in the law over and above that of the average citizen, the courts have said the group must "have been subjected to discrimination," and must "exhibit obvious, immutable or distinguishing characteristics that define them as a discrete group" and be "politically powerless."[2] The Supreme Court has defined as "immutable" such characteristics as "race, gender, or ethnic background," and "height or blindness."[3]

As far as being "politically powerless," homosexuals, who comprise less than 3 percent of the population, hardly lack wealth or political influence as a group. Even back in 2002, the National Journal found that homosexual activists have an outsized influence, using "their clout and their dollars to shape law and public policy."[4]

Not Comparable

Black Chicagoan Robert Oliver powerfully dismisses any comparison to what blacks have been through:

> When has a multitude of gays been kidnapped and made to be slaves for 400 years? When was it illegal to teach gays to read and write? When were there ever any gay Jim Crow laws? When were gays required to say 'sah' or 'ma'am' to straight people? When were there separated gay and straight water fountains? In public buildings, when were there separate entrances for gays and straights, the gays going out the back. . . .When were there segregated lunch counters based on sexual preference? When was a gay required to give up their seat on a bus to a straight person? Who was the gay Rosa Parks? Were gays at the bottom of the economic social structure for decades? Where were the poor gay ghettos? When have gays gotten worse jobs and lower pay

than straight people? When were there separate-but-equal schools for gays and straights?[5]

In recent years, transgender civil rights claims have exploded, as people who identify as the opposite sex demand the "right" to use restrooms and locker rooms that don't correspond to their birth sex. In 2016, in the "bathroom wars" in North Carolina, the city of Charlotte enacted an ordinance allowing transgendered persons to choose the opposite sex's restrooms. State lawmakers, reasoning that this was an abuse of civil rights law that trampled on privacy rights of other bathroom users, pushed back with a statewide bill overriding the Charlotte statute.

In response, corporations such as Deutsche Bank AG and PayPal canceled expansions, and many corporations announced boycotts of North Carolina, including General Electric, Dow Chemical Company, Pepsi, Hyatt, Hewlett Packard, Choice Hotels International, Whole Foods, Levi Strauss & Co., Lionsgate and others. Celebrities like Bruce Springsteen and Ringo Starr canceled concerts; the NCAA canceled its basketball tournament, and the National Basketball Association threatened to cancel its all-star game.[6] In March 2017, legislators rescinded the law, although they left in place a prohibition on cities creating their own LGBT non-discrimination laws until 2020.[7]

Similar pushbacks occurred in Arizona and Indiana, where legislators had passed laws designed to protect religious liberty only to retreat in the face of enormous corporate and media pressure.

The Nature of Civil Rights

Chai Feldblum, appointed by President Obama in a recess appointment to the Equal Employment Opportunity Commission has said, "Civil rights is a zero-sum game. Gays win, Christians lose." She is quite right about the enforcement of civil rights.[8] Many people think of civil rights as an ever-expanding tolerance, but the truth is that every claim of a civil right comes at the expense of another civil right. It is hierarchical with some goods trumping other goods. For example, Americans believe in the right to freedom of association. But we also believe that the right to do business without suffering discrimination trumps the freedom of association. It's also a fight between the right to obtain services and the right to freedom of expressive speech.

This issue is central, along with religious liberty, in the case of Christian florists, photographers, bakers, and wedding venue owners being charged with discrimination for declining to help facilitate same-sex ceremonies. The difference with other cases about denial of services is that it isn't about who the customer is—most of these businesses routinely sell their products or services to homosexual customers. It's about the event itself, which celebrates what God calls sin. For the same reason, some Christian bakers refuse to do Halloween cakes or risqué designs for bachelor parties. The competing rights here are freedom of religion versus freedom to obtain services.

> The Bible has little to say about rights, but a lot to say about duties—to God, to our families, to our communities, our nation and to the government (Caesar).

The Bible has little to say about rights, but a lot to say about duties—to God, to our families, to our communities, our nation and to the government (Caesar). Nonetheless, the theme of true liberty under God flows through the pages of both the Old and New Testaments, and it inspired America's Founders to adopt a Constitution that sharply limits government by assigning enumerated duties to the central (federal) government and the states while fencing off rights retained by the people.

The first and most important duty of government is to provide security. In return, people give up a certain degree of freedom (such as some of their income for taxes) to allow the state to assume the jurisdiction and resources necessary to maintain order.

In 1850, Frederic Bastiat identified legitimate government as the enforcer of the Law and explained it thusly:

> The law is the organization of the natural right of lawful defense. It is the substitution of a common force for individual forces. And this common force is to do only what the individual forces have a natural and lawful right to do: to protect persons, liberties, and properties; to maintain the right of each, and to cause justice to reign over us all.[9]

> The Bill of Rights lists individual rights and specific prohibitions on governmental power.

In addition to providing stability and the rule of law, government exists to protect other rights, some of which are stated specifically in the first 10 amendments to the Constitution, which are called the Bill of Rights.

The Constitution's prime drafter, James Madison, wrote the Bill of Rights because several states, fearing an overbearing central government, insisted on greater protection for individual liberties.

This mirrored Thomas Jefferson's concern. In the Kentucky Resolutions of 1798, he wrote: "[I]n questions of power then, let no more be heard of confidence in man, but bind him down from mischief by the chains of the constitution."[10]

Libertarian author Ayn Rand made a similar statement that has often been mistakenly credited to Mr. Jefferson: "There are two potential violators of man's rights: the criminals and the government. The great achievement of the United States was to draw a distinction between these two—by forbidding to the second the legalized version of the activities of the first."[11]

Bill of Rights: The Constitution's Safety Net

While the bulk of the Constitution assigns powers and duties of the various levels and branches of government, the Bill of Rights lists individual rights and specific prohibitions on governmental power:

- First Amendment: Freedom of religion, speech, press, assembly and petition.

- Second: Right to keep and bear arms.

- Third: No quartering of soldiers.

- Fourth: Freedom from unreasonable searches and seizures.

- Fifth: Right to due process of law, freedom from self-incrimination, double jeopardy.

- Sixth: Rights of accused persons, e.g., right to a speedy and public trial.

- Seventh: Right of trial by jury in civil cases.

- Eighth: Freedom from excessive bail, cruel and unusual punishments.

- Ninth: Other rights of the people.

- Tenth: Powers not delegated to the United States are reserved to the states and the people.

Over the years, the concept of civil rights gradually expanded. The biggest advance was the 13th Amendment (1865), which bans slavery, followed by the 15th Amendment (1870), which guarantees the right to vote regardless of race, and the 19th Amendment (1920) granting women the right to vote. The 23rd Amendment (1964) banned poll taxes on voters, and the 26th Amendment (1971) gave the vote to people 18 years of age and older.

In 1965, following passage the year before of the Civil Rights Act, the Jim Crow era ended with the Voting Rights Act and black Americans were restored to full citizenship in the United States after a century of legalized oppression. As the American Civil Rights Union (not to be confused with the American Civil Liberties Union) has stated:

> Jim Crow was an era in which whites, mostly but not always in the South, used methods sometimes legal, sometimes illegal, often deadly, but always immoral, to maintain political and cultural domination over blacks. Blacks were reduced to second-class citizenship. They were denied the right to vote, kept separate from whites in most phases of life, and in general, treated as if they were subhuman, in an effort to justify white supremacy and keep the black population under tight control.[12]

Restoring Real Civil Rights

With claims rising almost daily for newly coined "rights," it is paramount that we recover the original meaning of the "unalienable" rights that are the foundation of our liberty, and the legitimate expansions of civil rights that ended real discrimination.

Constitutional historian Charles Warren reminds us that, "however the Court may interpret the provisions of the Constitution, it is still the Constitution which is the law, not the decisions of the Court."[13]

Former Attorney General Edwin Meese III adds this perspective:

> By this, of course, Warren did not mean that a constitutional decision by the Supreme Court lacks the character of binding law. He meant that the Constitution remains the Constitution and that observers of the Court may fairly consider whether a particular Supreme Court decision was right or wrong.[14]

The Court has been deadly wrong on several occasions. In 1857, the Court ruled in the *Dred Scott* case that slaves who escaped to free states had to be returned to their owners in slave states.[15] It took the bloodiest war in U.S. history (the Civil War) to overturn the Court's glaring error.

In 1896, the Court issued a ruling in *Plessy v. Ferguson*[16] that established "separate but equal" facilities based on race. It took decades before other rulings such as *Brown v. Board of Education*[17] (1954) and legislation such as the Civil Rights Act of 1964 and Voting Rights Act of 1965 corrected the Court's unconstitutional mistakes. As Mr. Meese wrote:

"We have seen throughout our history that when the Supreme Court greatly misconstrues the Constitution, generations of mischief follow," wrote Mr. Meese. "The result is that, of its own accord or through the mechanism of the appointment process, the Supreme Court may come to revisit some of its doctrines and try, once again, to adjust its pronouncements to the commands of the Constitution."[18]

> "We have seen throughout our history that when the Supreme Court greatly misconstrues the Constitution, generations of mischief follow."
>
> Edwin Meese III

In recent years, the Court has erred greatly in crucial rulings, banning Bible reading and prayer in government schools,[19] legalizing abortion,[20] damaging property rights,[21] striking down the right of the people of Colorado to define civil rights classes according to traditional categories[22] and creating a heretofore unknown "right" to same-sex "marriage."[23]

Finding Balance

There is a profound sense that the Court has overstepped its role and has seized powers that the Founders never gave it.

In his dissent in the *Obergefell* same-sex "marriage" case, the late Justice Antonin Scalia wrote this:

> Today's decree says that my Ruler, and the Ruler of 320 million Americans coast-to-coast, is a majority of the nine lawyers on the Supreme Court. The opinion in these cases is the furthest extension in fact—and the furthest extension one can even imagine—of the Court's claimed power to create "liberties" that the Constitution and its Amendments neglect to mention. This practice of constitutional revision by an unelected committee of nine, always accompanied (as it is today) by extravagant praise of liberty, robs the People of the most important liberty they asserted in the Declaration of Independence and won in the Revolution of 1776: the freedom to govern themselves.[24]

The courts, and especially the Supreme Court, which have played a major role in distorting the true meaning of constitutional rights, also can be instruments of recovery if enough constitutionally-committed judges reach the bench.

What would America look like if real civil rights were enforced? A lot like 1950s America but without racial or ethnic discrimination. The military would seek out the most qualified to serve, not alter its standards to accommodate those who would hurt military readiness. Religious liberties would not be under assault from false civil rights claims.

In the *Masterpiece Cakeshop v. Colorado Civil Rights Commission* case, baker Jack Phillips asserts that he is a cake artist and that his creations are part of his glorifying God through his business. If the Supreme Court agrees, it will give life to First Amendment religious liberty protections and undo some of the damage of the *Obergefell* same-sex "marriage" ruling.

> What would America look like if real civil rights were enforced? A lot like 1950s America but without racial or ethnic discrimination.

A return to real civil rights will take the appointment of constitutionally sound judges at all levels, which appears to have begun under the Trump Administration. It will also take lawmakers and executive office holders, such as governors, asserting the primacy of the Constitution in their own spheres of power. They all take an oath to uphold it.

For all of this to happen, it will take an aroused voting populace reasserting the Constitution's clear direction as to who governs us—"We the people."

"But if anyone does not provide for his own, and especially for those of his household, he has denied the faith and is worse than an unbeliever."

— 1 Timothy 5:8

CHAPTER 6

From Redistribution to Economic Liberty

The Apostle Paul, who worked as a tentmaker to support himself, explicitly lays the duty on families themselves, and particularly on husbands and fathers, for meeting their families' needs.

Throughout the Proverbs, we are admonished that God is the ultimate source of our wellbeing, which includes our incomes: *"And my God shall supply all your need according to His riches in glory by Christ Jesus"* (Philippians 4:19).

We are also admonished to provide for widows and orphans. During Biblical times, they had far fewer opportunities to amass wealth on their own, but the principle holds today. The Bible's clear direction to share with those less blessed by material wealth is about real charitable giving, which aids the needy while blessing the giver.

By contrast, forced redistribution by government undermines the spirit of giving and corrupts recipients by breeding soul-destroying dependency. Plus, much of the federal redistribution

> Forced redistribution by government undermines the spirit of giving and corrupts recipients by breeding soul-destroying dependency.

63

apparatus may well be extra-legal. As a book title by Joseph Sobran proclaims, *Anything Called a "Program" Is Unconstitutional.*[1]

A Transfer of Responsibility

In 1935, Congress enacted the Social Security Act, which was pro-marriage and designed to support needy widows and their children. But the law also had unforeseen consequences for family relationships. It shifted responsibility from children who cared for aging parents to the government, that is, to other taxpayers.

While some people today spend much of their income to raise children, those children grow up to work and be taxed for the benefit of all, including those who decline to have children. As popular as Social Security has become, it was not supposed to be more than supplementary income for people saving for their own retirement. But, many people have failed to save and are entirely dependent on Social Security. A helping hand has become a lifeline.

> As popular as Social Security has become, it was not supposed to be more than supplementary income for people saving for their own retirement.

This is partly because people are living far longer than when Social Security was launched, and partly because government dependence has become ingrained in the American psyche as a "right."

The march toward government dependence began in earnest during the 1930s, when the Roosevelt Administration was struggling against the Great Depression. For perspective of what he was up against, consider the conditions after the Stock Market Crash of 1929:

> From late 1929 to early 1933, real economic output in the United States declined by 30 percent and unemployment grew from 3 percent to 25 percent. More than a third of the country's banks failed in

that period, leaving depositors broke and destroying much of the credit system.

Some of Roosevelt's early measures—deposit insurance, banking reform, and taking the U.S. off the gold standard—slowed the contraction but did not restore the economy to health. In 1938, the unemployment rate was still 17 percent. In 1940, on the eve of America's entry into World War II and as FDR ran for a third term, unemployment still hovered above 14 percent.[2]

Most historians, many of whom are liberals, credit Roosevelt's New Deal with bringing America out of the Depression. While it was really the war that finally broke the back of the ruinous recession, it is also evident that Roosevelt's many programs and actions gave Americans hope that economic stability could be restored within the framework of constitutional government, or at least a facsimile thereof. But the price was high: a great leap toward socialism.

In her book *The Forgotten Man: A New History of the Great Depression*, journalist Amity Shlaes "argues persuasively that a key to [Franklin] Roosevelt's success was his mastery of the political process and especially his knack for passing legislation that would create constituent groups henceforth supportive of Democratic candidates," writes James Piereson. He continues:

> These included senior citizens mobilized by the Social Security Act, unions by the Wagner Act, artists and intellectuals by the Works Progress Administration, farmers by agricultural subsidies, and consumers by the promise of cheap electrical power.
>
> The creation of large constituencies for federal programs was a new development in the United States, one that ran against the grain of established

practices of federalism and private enterprise. Indeed, during the founding era, Jefferson and Madison had feared precisely this prospect in their battles with Hamilton over federal power. Yet this was surely one of the more significant legacies of the New Deal.[3]

Ratchet forward to the mid-1960s, when Lyndon Johnson unleashed the Great Society's "War on Poverty." While it helped some people, it also made life much worse in the inner cities all over America by destroying incentives for marriage and encouraging out-of-wedlock births. If a pregnant girl got married, she would give up many welfare benefits, so household income alone dissuaded many couples from tying the knot.

From 1960 to 1964, two-thirds of black babies were born into married households.[4] By 2015, that number had fallen to less than 30 percent for blacks, and less than 60 percent for women of all races.[5] In some cities, single mothers comprise more than 80 percent of black births.

The result of the rampant rise in fatherless homes has been shockingly clear: increases in crime, drug and alcohol abuse, child abuse, gang violence and chronic dependency.[6]

The Welfare Trap

Over the years, the number of federal anti-poverty programs has grown to more than 75 agencies that "provide cash, food, housing, medical care, and social services to poor and low-income persons."[7]

"These means-tested programs—including food stamps, public housing, low-income energy assistance, and Medicaid—pay the bills and meet the physical needs of tens of millions of low-income families. However, these programs do not help the recipients move from a position of dependence on the government to being able to provide for themselves," the Heritage Foundation reports.[8]

"Only one welfare program, Temporary Assistance for Needy

Families (TANF), promotes greater self-reliance. The reform that created TANF in the mid-1990s moved 2.8 million families off the welfare rolls and into jobs so that they were providing for themselves."⁹

Beginning in 1996, large, finite chunks of federal agency money under TANF were block granted to the states so that solutions could be found at the state and local levels. Congress also inserted work requirements for welfare recipients.

> Over the years, the number of federal anti-poverty programs has grown to more than 75 agencies that "provide cash, food, housing, medical care, and social services to poor and low-income persons.

Gone was the incentive to keep adding people to the welfare rolls in order to get more federal money. Gone were the dictates flowing from Washington.

TANF differed radically from the program it replaced, Aid to Families with Dependent Children. Under AFDC, states got more money for each new person enrolled—an incentive to increase their welfare rolls.

From 1965 to 1996, these unconditional welfare entitlements had the effect of shunting aside fathers by giving mothers numerous cash incentives to stay single. The result was a decrease in marriages and a soaring rate of out-of-wedlock births, as noted above.

Under the TANF block grant, federal funding remains the same regardless of caseload. If states reduce their rolls, they can use the savings for enhanced services such as child care or transportation, for the remaining low-income persons who may be harder to train or prepare for employment.

"This simple fix shifted the mindset of state agencies from an emphasis on increasing enrollment and processing checks to a new focus on shrinking caseloads and increasing employment," according to the Carleson Center for Welfare Reform.[10]

The system shifted back toward dependency in 2012, when President Obama issued a memorandum encouraging states to apply for exemptions from the longstanding work participation standards.[11]

"To do this, the Obama administration claimed waiver authority that was illegal and antithetical to the purpose," wrote Heritage Foundation welfare experts Robert Rector and Vijay Menon. "President Barack Obama's Department of Health and Human Services produced no historical evidence that Congress intended to grant waiver authority for the TANF work requirements."[12]

Restoring Economic Liberty

A return to constitutional governance begins with the principle of subsidiarity, in which social responsibility begins in the home, extends to the extended family, then the church, neighbors and the community and on up through the various governments.

Instead of dictating from the top down, subsidiarity governance is closer to the people and therefore more responsive. If you don't think so, compare calling a local council member with a problem with calling one of the numberless bureaucrats in one of Washington's bloated federal agencies. Good luck, especially on a Friday afternoon.

In August 2017, the Trump Administration reinstated the work requirements for welfare with HHS officials explaining that, "Our agency is committed to helping low-income families transition from welfare to work. We cannot achieve the goal of self-sufficiency if meaningful work participation is divorced from welfare cash assistance."[13]

> "We should measure welfare's success by how many people leave welfare, not by how many are added."
>
> Ronald Reagan

As President Ronald Reagan eloquently put it, welfare's purpose is "to provide for the needy, of course, but more than that, to salvage these, our fellow citizens, to make them self-sustaining and, as quickly as possible, independent of welfare. We should measure welfare's success by how many people leave welfare, not by how many are added."[14]

Indeed, the most effective charity in America—the Salvation Army—requires "work therapy" and other training that encourages aid recipients to get out of dependency. Being a Christian denomination, the Salvation Army also emphasizes God's plan for marriage and family.

Ultimately, the best solution and one that would meet constitutional muster would be to send far less tax money to D.C. in the first place, cut back federal programs, and add incentives for churches and other charities to regain their status as first responders to people in need.

> The most effective charity in America—the Salvation Army—requires "work therapy" and other training that encourages aid recipients to get out of dependency.

By cutting the government, taxes could also be cut, allowing families to keep more of their hard-earned income and allowing businesses more revenue for expansion.

Reforming Social Security

Each year, millions of Baby Boomers are retiring and drawing Social Security payments. The problem is that in 1935, there were 16 employees for every beneficiary, and people's average lifespan was far lower. Now there are only four workers per Social Security recipient, and it is headed toward a 2 to 1 ratio, even as lifespans have lengthened.[15]

The same problems confront Medicare and Medicaid. So, what are the solutions? For starters, the system must be retained for current beneficiaries or those who are about to receive benefits. You don't yank the rug out from under people who had no choice but to participate in the system.

But a few reforms could put Social Security on a better footing so that it is there for future recipients.

The retirement age can be raised gradually to 70, given that peo-

> A return to constitutional governance would mean the diminishment or even the end of many federal initiatives and a rebirth of personal responsibility.

ple live and work longer. Secondly, Social Security was sold as a sort of insurance program, but it has become a welfare system for older Americans. Means-testing may be in order at a certain bracket. Also, younger Americans should be able to direct some of their income in investment accounts that can vary according to risk.

Likewise, people should be able to have pretax dollars flow into health savings accounts, an idea championed by former presidential candidate and now HUD Secretary Ben Carson, one of the nation's top neurosurgeons.

As Ken Blackwell and Ken Klukowski argue in *Resurgent: How Constitutional Conservatism Can Save America*:

> Overhauling Social Security and Medicare gets back to the keys of constitutional conservatism... By educating Americans on how to be self-sufficient and giving them the means to act on this knowledge, we can move back toward a culture of individualism and family, instead of one in which the government is the center of our universe, on which we rely for our daily bread.[16]

A return to constitutional governance would mean the diminishment or even the end of many federal initiatives and a rebirth of personal responsibility.

While encouraging us to trust God for our provision, the Bible is also clear that we should work hard and wisely manage our money.

> *Go to the ant, you sluggard! Consider her ways and be wise, which, having no captain, overseer or ruler,*

provides her supplies in the summer, and gathers her food in the harvest (Proverbs 6: 6-8).

For those who work for a living, the government needs to get out of the way and stop confiscating so much of people's hard-earned income. In addition to putting an end to disincentives to work, we need tax reform that rewards instead of punishes those who play by the rules.

"Each of us has a natural right—from God—to defend his person, his liberty, and his property. These are the three basic requirements of life, and the preservation of any one of them is completely dependent upon the preservation of the other two. For what are our faculties but the extension of our individuality? And what is property but an extension of our faculties?" [1]

— Frederic Bastiat

CHAPTER 7

Taxation with Representation

One way to look at taxes is through the lens of coercion. That is, the understanding that taxes are not voluntary contributions but are backed by the force of government.

Humorist P.J. O'Rourke explains it in his "gray-haired mother" routine:

> All tax revenue is the result of holding a gun to somebody's head. Not paying taxes is against the law. If you don't pay your taxes you'll be fined. If you don't pay the fine, you'll be jailed. If you try to escape from jail you'll be shot. Thus I—in my role as citizen and voter—am going to shoot you in your role as taxpayer . . . if you don't pay your share of the national tab. Therefore, every time the government spends money on anything you have to ask yourself: Would I kill my kindly, gray-haired mother for this?[2]

Comedy aside, Mr. O'Rourke has a serious point. Whenever the government imposes a tax, it is with the understanding that you will go to jail

> The government has an obligation to spend (your taxes) wisely.

or worse if you do not pay it. Therefore, the government has an obligation to spend it wisely. If it does not do so or is functionally not accountable, it amounts to taxation without representation.

"Government is not reason, it is not eloquence—it is force. Like fire it is a dangerous servant and a fearful master," George Washington allegedly declared, though it may be apocryphal; modern scholarship has not turned up an original source.[3] But the statement is quoted often because it epitomizes the founders' thinking.

At the very least, since government can take away our freedom merely by enforcing tax law, we should, as a self-governing people, carefully choose the representatives who do the taxing and spending.

In 1761, James Otis, a Massachusetts lawyer and a member of the colony's provincial assembly, coined the phrase "taxation without representation is tyranny" to decry the American colonists' plight of being subjected to levies by a British parliament that had no elected American representatives.[4]

It became the rallying cry for America's revolutionaries, some of whom converted it into "no taxation without representation."

When French economist Frederic Bastiat wrote his masterpiece *The Law* in 1850, it was two years after a second French revolution was pushing France into outright socialism. Bastiat's essay acknowledges the necessity of government as a collective protector of people's life and property, along with their natural rights. Taxation, he argued, is unavoidable—but only to fund minimal state functions. Anything more than that, he famously wrote, amounts to "plunder."

He opens with this:

> We hold from God the gift which includes all others. This gift is—physical, intellectual, and moral life.
>
> But life cannot maintain itself alone. The Creator of life has entrusted us with the responsibility of preserving, developing, and perfecting it. In order that we may accomplish this, He has provided us

TAXATION WITH REPRESENTATION

with a collection of marvelous faculties. And He has put us in the midst of a variety of natural resources. By the application of our faculties to these natural resources we convert them into products, and use them. This process is necessary in order that life may run its appointed course.

Life, faculties, production—in other words, individuality, liberty, property—this is man. And, in spite of the cunning of artful political leaders, these three gifts from God precede all human legislation, and are superior to it. Life, liberty, and property do not exist because men have made laws. On the contrary, it was the fact that life, liberty, and property existed beforehand that caused men to make laws in the first place.

What, then, is law? It is the collective organization of the individual right to lawful defense.

The United States of America began with a revolt over a government that had turned on its subjects, imposing oppressive taxation. King George III's English government was insisting on taxing everything in sight through the dreaded "stamp tax," in which colonists had to buy stamps to show that they had paid taxes of one kind or another.

In the Constitution's Article I—the section that establishes the powers of Congress—federal lawmakers are authorized to "lay and collect taxes."

Tariffs on foreign goods were the principal federal tax, which was shared with the states. There was no income tax until 1861, when it was imposed to help pay for the Civil War.

> The United States of America began with a revolt over a government that had turned on its subjects, imposing oppressive taxation.

75

After the tax lapsed, the Supreme Court struck down all attempts to make the tax permanent, that is, until passage of the 16th Amendment in 1913.

"After ratification, President Woodrow Wilson pushed for passage of the Revenue Act of 1913, which lowered tariffs on foreign goods from 40 percent to 25 percent, and instituted a graduated income tax," Dr. Karen Gushta wrote in her book, *How Can America Survive? The Coming Economic Earthquake*. "Within a few years, the income tax became the primary source of revenue for the federal government. The door was open for the expansion of big government...."[5]

And grow it did. By 2018, thanks to both Democrat and Republican Congresses and presidential administrations, the national debt reached more than $20 trillion.

> By 2018, thanks to both Democrat and Republican Congresses and presidential administrations, the national debt reached more than $20 trillion.

A sobering way to assess the sheer growth of government spending is to take a look at the U.S. National Debt Clock, which can be found online at usdebtclock.org. Introduced on February 20, 1989 by New York real estate magnate Seymour Durst, the U.S. National Debt Clock began by reporting a national debt of "only" $2.7 trillion. By 1991, it was ticking upward at $13,000 per second. "The amount began accumulating so fast that the last seven digits became totally illegible," Time magazine reported.[6]

The clock, which was mounted on a building near 42nd Street in Manhattan, stopped in 1995 during a government shutdown. (See, gridlock is good.) That was the same year Mr. Durst died. The clock got going again under his son, Douglas, but broke in 1998 when its computers couldn't handle the total of $5.5 trillion.

With new hardware, the clock continued to tick upward until September 7, 2000, when it actually began going backwards due to the wonderful fact that the national debt began decreasing. If you're a Democrat, you might credit the Clinton administration. If you're a Republican, you might instead credit Newt Gingrich and the GOP Congress for slapping a lid on Mr. Clinton's capacious spending plans.

In any case, that rare period ended with the dot-com crash and the economic fallout from 9/11, and the Durst Organization cranked the clock back up in 2002.

"By 2008, they had to revamp it yet again, adding a digit, because the Bush Administration had nearly doubled the debt to $10 trillion. Over the next eight years, the Obama Administration's annual deficits (with the Republican House's complicity from 2011 on and the full GOP Congress from 2015 on) managed to double it again. As of [February 2018], the national debt [was] cruising beyond $20.6 trillion."[7]

The Real Cost

There is an extremely important moral component to piling up this much debt. Someone will have to pay it someday. That means we are spending money that hasn't even been earned yet by our children, grandchildren and great-grandchildren.

In 2 Corinthians 12:14b, Paul admonishes that *"the children ought not to lay up for the parents, but the parents for the children."* Our accumulating national debt is the opposite.

Tom Paine, whose fiery essays preceding the American Revolution were the most-read treatises in the colonies other than the Bible, wrote of the immorality of saddling subsequent generations with bad laws, whose corollary is bad debt:

> Every age and generation must be free to act for itself in all cases as the age and generations which preceded it. The vanity and presumption of governing beyond the grave is the most ridiculous and insolent of all tyrannies.[8]

"Taxation without representation" is exactly what our deficit spending is doing to the next generations. They have no say whatever in their economic bondage.

By granting so much power to the federal government, we have, in effect, denied self-governance to our posterity. That on its face violates the promise of the Constitution's Preamble to "secure the Blessings of Liberty to ourselves and our Posterity."

Disenfranchising the Ones Who Pay the Taxes

Taxing honest work while rewarding indolence is the game plan for secular progressives who wish to radically transform America into a place where everyone is dependent on government for our subsistence. This is antithetical to what the Bible teaches about economic independence within the framework of dependency on God alone.

As government grows at the executive level—the many federal agencies that have tens of thousands of employees who issue thousands of pages of regulations—the levers of real power are getting farther from the people.

"The administrative state has made the current U.S. government almost unrecognizable to what the Founders envisioned," wrote historian and Hoover Institution Fellow Victor Davis Hanson.[9] The result is less freedom and more government coercion.

"Any system that denies individuals the right to make their own economic decisions is denying them the freedom to pursue their dreams, aspirations, and calling," wrote Dr. Gushta. "Since each person's gifts, talents, native bent, and calling are uniquely God-given, any political regime that seeks to make everyone 'equal' in terms of the outcomes of their efforts is at its root unbiblical and ungodly."[10]

One way to think about taxes is to consider that slavery is 100 percent taxation of someone's labor. So, if government at all levels combined is taking nearly 50 percent of our earnings, we are half slaves. Since the LORD asks a tithe of our incomes (as a minimal contribution), it seems arrogant of government to ask for much more than 10 percent. When Jesus instructed the Pharisees to give "to Caesar the things that are Caesar's, and to God the things that are God's," He did not add that Caesar should get the lion's share.

The drive toward government-facilitated economic "equality" sometimes coughs up odd experiments that defy human nature and what we know from history. The colonists at Jamestown (1607) and at Plymouth (1620) nearly starved before halting their fling with communism and instituting a system of private property and free enterprise.

> "Since each person's gifts, talents, native bent, and calling are uniquely God-given, any political regime that seeks to make everyone 'equal' in terms of the outcomes of their efforts is at its root unbiblical and ungodly."
>
> Dr. Karen Gushta

In January 2018, the mayor of Stockton, California, a city that went bankrupt in 2012, announced that the city would provide a "Universal Basic Income" to some of the city's poor.[11] The idea is to give them money—$500 per family—with no strings attached, and see what happens.

"I think it will make people work better and smarter and harder," Mayor Michael Tubbs told National Public Radio.[12]

Some of the funds will come from a left-wing foundation—the Economic Security Project[13]—that wants to study the "economic and social impacts" on people getting free money. Especially important to the researchers will be the impacts on their "self-esteem and identity," according to Fox News.[14]

"It's only going to be an experiment with 'several dozen families,' for starters," wrote veteran journalist and Christian author Lee Duigon. "But [Mr. Tubbs] is hoping it'll be fantastically successful and will inspire other cities to do likewise—with lots and lots of 'families.' I put 'families' in quotes because I really don't know what a Democrat means by the word 'families' anymore."[15]

As to the overall effect, "Nothing is said of the potential impact on the poor [taxpayers] who will have to keep on working while the layabout next door collects $6,000 a year for playing video games and producing out-of-wedlock children," Mr. Duigon comments. "Do you think it might be just a tad demoralizing?"

Back to the Constitutional Promise

How do we address the immoral situation in which we find ourselves—being overly taxed by an unresponsive and often irresponsible government intent on redistribution over freedom? The short answer is: by reining in spending, cutting back on government regulations and shifting power back to the states and the people, respectively.

To do that we need leaders of substance who are steeped in Biblical values and are willing to work to see these values embodied in sound public policy. We also need a populace steeped in Biblical values; those who do not need an overweening government to manage them. That will take a revival of enormous magnitude.

"Too often we forget that America became a nation soon after a spiritual revival, the First Great Awakening," Dr. D. James Kennedy said on the steps of the Lincoln Memorial in 2003. "Then in the 1800s, America experienced a Second Great Awakening, which helped bring about a moral revolution—particularly in addressing the evil of slavery. But now we are in need of a Third Great Awakening."[16]

> "Too often we forget that America became a nation soon after a spiritual revival, the First Great Awakening."
>
> D. James Kennedy

The only way that Americans will reverse the slide toward bigger and less accountable government will be more citizens capable of self-governance who can hold lawmakers accountable as their representatives instead of their masters.

"Many are under the misconception that government will solve all our problems," Dr. Kennedy said. "But I believe that true change is going to take place when people throughout the nation begin to trust in Christ and in the God that made this nation great. And that will bring about a genuine revival—a revival that eventually moves to the halls of government. Not from the government down, but from the people up."

In the meantime, Christians and others need to take a more active role in the election process, either as candidates, election workers, poll watchers, or as voters. They need to be informed by seeking out evidence that reveals where their would-be representatives will take them.

As Dr. Kennedy summarized, "For whom should Christians vote? For those who embrace their moral, spiritual, and political values as informed by the Scriptures."[17]

Frederic Bastiat wrote that the key to liberty is not good intentions but a reduction in government power:

> And now that the legislators and do-gooders have so futilely inflicted so many systems upon society, may they finally end where they should have begun: May they reject all systems, and try liberty; for liberty is an acknowledgment of faith in God and His works.[18]

"We in America have been given a great inheritance. No other previous nation in history has had a constitution guaranteeing that its people could freely live out their religion without government interference. In a nation settled by the belief that the government's only real job is to secure our God-given freedoms, it would be an unimaginable tragedy if "we the people" were to let such a heritage slip through our fingers."

— JOHN RABE[1]

CHAPTER 8

Restoring a Constitutional Form of Government

It's no accident that in the handwritten copy of the Constitution, the Preamble begins with *We the People* in larger letters than the rest of the text.

The government exists to serve the people, not the other way around, as is the case, sadly, in many authoritarian and totalitarian nations.

In recent years, the Preamble has been misused, however, as an excuse to expand federal power. Here it is, in its entirety:

> Although the Preamble outlines the broad objectives of the federal government, it does not confer any authority whatever.

"We the People of the United States, in Order to form a more perfect Union, establish Justice, insure domestic Tranquility, provide for the common defence, promote the general Welfare, and secure the Blessings of Liberty to ourselves and our Posterity, do ordain and establish this Constitution for the United States of America."

Although the Preamble outlines the broad objectives of the federal government, it does not confer any authority whatever. That is left to the articles that list the various powers of each branch and of the states.

Despite the clear direction from the Founders that the Constitution is to serve as a check on government, the phrases "promote the general Welfare, and secure the Blessings of Liberty" have been used as blank checks to justify virtually any expansion of power.

When the Affordable Care Act was being debated in October 2009, a reporter asked House Speaker Nancy Pelosi what part of the Constitution gave the federal government the authority to enact an individual health insurance mandate.

"Are you serious? Are you serious?" she famously answered with a laugh,[2] which many people interpreted as disdain for constitutional limitations on federal power.

So how do we get back to a constitutional republic with limited government power?

As with any venture, we must start with prayer. We can do nothing without the help of Almighty God.

Psalm 127:1 states, *"Except the Lord build the house, they labor in vain who build it..."*

It was precisely because God was forgotten that we have drifted so far toward a government of men instead of laws.

On June 2, 1979, the world witnessed a stunning event. A Polish-born Pope, John Paul II, arose in Victory Square in communist-ruled Warsaw to give a sermon that effectively spelled the end of the Cold War.

> Psalm 127:1 states, "Except the Lord build the house, they labor in vain who build it..."

A million of his countrymen listened to this remarkable man openly pray and extol the goodness of God and the saving power of Jesus Christ. He did so in a country where in 1939, Nazi tanks rolled across Poland's Western border. They were followed 16 days later by Soviet tanks invading from the East, and thousands of Poles were massacred. Under Soviet rule, over the next four decades thousands more were jailed, tortured, or executed for the crime of sharing their Christian faith.

> America has been uniquely blessed by God as the freest, most prosperous nation in history. But we are at a crossroads.

So, while John Paul II was giving his sermon, the energized crowd, desperate for freedom after years of misery, erupted in a chant of "We want God! We want God! We want God!"[3]

In 2017, another heartening historic event occurred in Warsaw that was either mocked or ignored by much of the American media. President Donald Trump spoke in Krasinski Square on July 8 to tens of thousands of Poles, praising them for their indomitable spirit, unquenched faith, and their Western values rooted in Christianity. Recounting the Pope's historic 1979 appearance, Mr. Trump said,

> Every communist in Warsaw must have known that their oppressive system would soon come crashing down. They must have known it at the exact moment during Pope John Paul II's sermon when a million Polish men, women and children suddenly raised their voices in a single prayer. A million Polish people did not ask for wealth. They did not ask for privileges. Instead, one million Poles sang three simple words: 'We Want God!'[4]

King Solomon, when asked by God what he wanted upon ascending to the throne of Israel, did not seek power or riches, but the wisdom to rule his people in a Godly way. For this, God made him the wisest man in history—for as long as he stayed faithful. There is a lesson here for our own country.

America has been uniquely blessed by God as the freest, most prosperous nation in history. But we are at a crossroads. We are either going to succumb to the moral bankruptcy of relativism and secularism, or we are going to experience a Christian awakening and turn back to God. There's nothing in between.

Sometimes, although it seems that darkness is gaining, bright lights arise that the darkness does not know how to answer.

> We are either going to succumb to the moral bankruptcy of relativism and secularism, or we are going to experience a Christian awakening and turn back to God. There's nothing in between.

When the underdog Philadelphia Eagles won their first Super Bowl, defeating the heavily favored New England Patriots by a score of 41 to 33 on February 4, 2018, Eagles coach Doug Pederson had a microphone thrust in his face and was asked what it meant to him. With literally hundreds of millions of people around the globe watching him, he said, "I can only give the praise to my Lord and Savior Jesus Christ for giving me this opportunity." Then he credited his players for their will to win.

Eagles Quarterback Nick Foles, who was named Most Valuable Player, also had the opportunity to say anything he wanted. So, holding his baby daughter Lily, he did: "All glory to God. Lily really likes this mic. She has no idea," the MVP said. . . . "To be here with my daughter, my wife, my teammates, this city . . . we're very blessed."[5] On other occasions, Mr. Foles has made no secret of his strong Christian faith.

Although the National Football League was plagued during 2017 with players who would not stand for the national anthem, reports of domestic violence, and declining attendance and viewership, many Christian players and coaches left a deep impact on the public.

The more that Christians with a platform speak out and

unapologetically express their faith and their love of country, the more that average Americans take heart and fight back against the Left's relentless campaign to radically transform America. Bravery is infectious.

"I believe a time is coming and soon will be upon us when we shall return to that vision of the Founders of America. Christians should be encouraged," wrote Dr. D. James Kennedy.

> We should be encouraged to realize that we are not losing, and defeated, and discouraged, and marginalized. Rather, just the opposite is true.
>
> We need to realize we can make a difference—we can make determinative difference in the direction of this country. We have had forty years of secular humanistic principles imposed upon this country, and these principles have delivered chaos and corruption. I think American Christians are waking up to say, "Enough is enough! We are going to change America back to what it once was."[6]

We do not need a majority in order to turn America back to its legacy of a Constitution designed to facilitate ordered liberty. We need a committed minority, and that will take activating more courageous pastors who in turn will activate their congregations to be salt and light in their communities.

We need to get out the vote, run for office, vote for honest, effective lawmakers, and press our public officials to appoint judges who respect the Constitution.

President Donald Trump's first Supreme Court appointment of a constitutional conservative, Neil Gorsuch, appears to have already borne fruit. Seated on April 10, 2017, Justice Gorsuch has voted consistently as a strict originalist. That means he takes the Constitution as written and not how it has been twisted by courts over the years.

"During his short tenure so far on the bench," wrote constitutional attorney Ken Klukowski, "Gorsuch has proven himself a strictly principled jurist who had not deviated even once from the original public meaning of any provision in the Constitution or federal law."[7]

We have seen the difference that God-fearing people who understand the battle can make when placed in positions of influence and office.

There is no magic formula for reducing government and restoring constitutional law. It will be a long-term struggle, but one that is well worth undertaking. The best hope for America—and the world—is a growing Christian community that seeks God's will and acts accordingly at all levels.

"We want God" needs to be on our lips and in our hearts.

Only when we are capable of self-governance can we throw off the chains of those who would be our overseers. That takes bending our knee to God through Jesus Christ. When we do so, we no longer have to bend it to any mere man or woman.

ENDNOTES

CHAPTER 1 — From Abuse of "Free Expression" Back to Real Free Speech

1. D. James Kennedy, "Liberty or License," sermon at Coral Ridge Presbyterian Church, Fort Lauderdale, FL, May 11, 1986.
2. Edwin Meese III, Matthew Spalding, David F. Forte, "The Heritage Guide to the Constitution," (Washington, D.C.: The Heritage Foundation, 2005), p. 314.
3. Ibid.
4. *Masterpiece Cake Shop, Ltd. v. Colorado Civil Rights Commission*, argued Dec. 5, 2017, at: http://www.scotusblog.com/case-files/cases/masterpiece-cakeshop-ltd-v-colorado-civil-rights-commn/
5. David Lowenthal, *No Liberty for License: The Forgotten Logic of the First Amendment*, (Dallas: Spence Publishing Company, 1997), p. 94.
6. Ibid, p. 95.
7. Ibid, p. 96.
8. Ibid, p. 97.
9. *Roth v. United States* 354 U.S. 476 (1957).
10. Ibid, p. 99.
11. See Dr. Judith A. Reisman and Edward W. Eichel, *Kinsey, Sex and Fraud*, Huntington House Publishers (Lafayette, La.: 1990); Judith A. Reisman, Ph.D., *Sexual Sabotage*, (Washington, D.C.: WND Books, 2010).
12. Alfred A. Kinsey, Wardell B. Pomeroy, Clyde R. Martin, *Sexual Behavior in the Human Male*, (Philadelphia: W.B. Saunders Co., 1948); Alfred C. Kinsey and the staff at the Institute for Sex Research, Indiana University, *Sexual Behavior in the Human Female*, (Philadelphia: W. B. Saunders Co., 1953).
13. Dr. Judith A. Reisman, *Kinsey: Crimes and Consequences*, (Crestwood, KY.: Institute for Media Education, 1998; 2000), pp. 187-260.
14. Ibid.
15. Ibid, p. 205.
16. James H. Jones, *Alfred C. Kinsey: A Public/Private Life*, (New York: W.W. Norton and Co., 1997), pp. 13-15.
17. Quoted in Lowenthal, p. 128.
18. Ibid, p. 129.
19. William O. Douglas, opinion in *A Book Named "John Cleland's Memoirs of a Woman of Pleasure" v. Massachusetts* (1966), 383 U.S. 413, 431, cited in Lowenthal, p. 93.

20 Lowenthal, p. 136.

21 *Paris Adult Theatre I v. Slaton* 413 U.S. 49 (1973).

22 *Miller v. California* 413 U.S. 15 (1973).

23 Warren Burger, quoted in Lowenthal, p. 139.

24 Patrick Trueman, email to author, January 5, 2018.

25 Robert Charles Winthrop, speech to the annual meeting of the Massachusetts Bible Society, May 28, 1849, cited in William J. Federer, *America's God and Country Encyclopedia of Quotations*, (St. Louis: Amerisearch, 2000), p. 702.

CHAPTER 2 — Restoring Respect for Life

1 Sadly, slavery is still practiced in many nations. Walk Free Foundation's Global Slavery Index is at: https://www.globalslaveryindex.org. According to Gallup surveys of 167 countries, there about 40 million slaves worldwide in 2017. See also Josh Gelernter, "Slavery Still Exists – We Just Don't Talk about It," *National Review*, June 4, 2016, at: http://www.nationalreview.com/article/436205/slavery-still-exists

2 Michael Schwartz, *The Supreme Court versus The American Family*, (Milwaukee: The Catholic League for Religious and Civil Rights, 1983), pp. 1-4.

3 *Griswold v. Connecticut* 381 U.S. 479 (1965).

4 Ibid, p. 7.

5 *Eisenstadt v. Baird* 405 U.S. 438 (1972).

6 *Roe v. Wade* 410 U.S. 113 (1973).

7 *Doe v. Bolton* 410 U.S. 179 (1973).

8 Schwartz, p. 10.

9 Danielle Paquette, "Why Abortion Clinics in the U.S. Are Rapidly Closing," *The Washington Post*, Feb. 25, 2016, at: https://www.washingtonpost.com/news/wonk/wp/2016/02/25/why-americas-abortion-clinics-are-rapidly-closing/?utm_term=.5fb58cdca25f

10 Joel Mowbray, "Did Obama Lie about the Born Alive Bill?" *RealClearPolitics.com*, August 21, 2008, at: https://www.realclearpolitics.com/articles/2008/08/did_obama_lie_about_born_alive.html

11 "Reported Annual Abortions," Fact Sheet, National Right to Life Committee, at: https://www.nrlc.org/uploads/factsheets/FS01AbortionintheUS.pdf. See also Sarah McCammon, "U.S. Abortion Rate Falls to Lowest Level Since Roe v. Wade," National Public Radio, January 17, 2017, at: https://www.npr.org/sections/thetwo-way/2017/01/17/509734620/u-s-abortion-rate-falls-to-lowest-level-since-roe-v-wade

12   Paquette, op. cit.

13   John D. Hagen, Jr., "The Crisis of Crisis Pregnancy Centers: Attacks on Them Deform the First Amendment," *The Weekly Standard*, September 22, 2017, at: http://www.weeklystandard.com/crisis-pregnancy-centers-in-crisis/article/2009771

14   Planned Parenthood Annual Report 2016-2017, cited in Nicole Russell, "If the GOP controls the government, why does Planned Parenthood still get federal funding?" *Washington Examiner*, January 8, 2018, at: http://www.washingtonexaminer.com/if-the-gop-controls-the-government-why-does-planned-parenthood-still-get-federal-funding/article/2645291

CHAPTER 3 — Federalism vs. Federal Control

1   Joseph Sobran, "How Tyranny Came to America," Sobran's, undated, at: http://www.sobran.com/articles/tyranny.shtml

2   Ken Blackwell, Ken Klukowski, *Resurgent: How Constitutional Conservatism Can Save America* (New York: Threshold Editions, Simon & Schuster, 2011), p. 120.

3   *Washington v. Gluckberg*, 521 U.S. 702, 720-21 (1997), cited in *Resurgent*, p. 120.

4   Jay Cost, "The Expanding Power of the Presidency," a review of Mitchel A. Sollenberger's and Mark J. Rozell's book *The President's Czars: Undermining Congress and the Constitution*, October/November 2012 Policy Review, the Hoover Institution, Stanford University, October 2, 2012, at: https://www.hoover.org/research/expanding-power-presidency

5   "What Is the Total U.S. Government Revenue?" February 2018, U.S. Government Revenue, at: https://www.usgovernmentrevenue.com/current_revenue

6   Edwin Meese, et al, *The Heritage Guide to the Constitution* (Washington, D.C.: Regnery Publishing, 2005), p. 291.

7   Charles Pinckney proposed this, but was rebuffed. Source: *Heritage Guide*.

8   James Madison, *Federalist 45*, Congress.gov Resources, at: https://www.congress.gov/resources/display/content/The+Federalist+Papers#TheFederalistPapers-45

CHAPTER 4 — The Road Back to Natural Marriage

1   *Washington v. Gluckberg* 521 U.S. 702, 720-21 (1997), cited in *Resurgent*, p. 120.

2   William Blackstone, *Commentaries*, Introduction, cited in "William Blackstone" under "What Are the Principles of the Commentaries?" pp. 40-41, Blackstone Institute, at: http://www.blackstoneinstitute.org/_oldsite/sirwilliamblackstone.html

3   "William Blackstone," p. 1.

4   http://www.scotusblog.com/case-files/cases/masterpiece-cakeshop-ltd-v-

colorado-civil-rights-commn/

5   Thomas Jefferson, the Virginia Statute of Religious Freedom. The context: "Well aware that the opinions and belief of men depend not on their own will, but follow involuntarily the evidence proposed to their minds; that Almighty God hath created the mind free, and manifested his supreme will that free it shall remain by making it altogether insusceptible of restraint; that all attempts to influence it by temporal punishments, or burthens, or by civil incapacitations, tend only to beget habits of hypocrisy and meanness, and are a departure from the plan of the holy author of our religion, who being lord both of body and mind, yet chose not to propagate it by coercions on either, as was in his Almighty power to do, but to extend it by its influence on reason alone; that the impious presumption of legislators and rulers, civil as well as ecclesiastical, who, being themselves but fallible and uninspired men, have assumed dominion over the faith of others, setting up their own opinions and modes of thinking as the only true and infallible, and as such endeavoring to impose them on others, hath established and maintained false religions over the greatest part of the world and through all time: That to compel a man to furnish contributions of money for the propagation of opinions which he disbelieves and abhors, is sinful and tyrannical." at: https://www.monticello.org/site/research-and-collections/virginia-statute-religious-freedom

6   Helen Alvare, "Symposium: As a matter of marriage law, wedding cake is expressive conduct," *Scotusblog*, Sept. 13, 2017, at: http://www.scotusblog.com/2017/09/symposium-matter-marriage-law-wedding-cake-expressive-conduct/

7   *Baehr v. Lewin* 852 P.2d 44 (Haw. 1993).

8   *Romer v. Evans* 517 U.S. 620 (1996).

9   *Romer v. Evans* at: http://caselaw.lp.findlaw.com/scripts/getcase.pl?court=US&vol=000&invol=u10179

10 *Lawrence v. Texas* 539 U.S. 558 (2003).

11 Dr. D. James Kennedy, "The Importance of Marriage," sermon at Coral Ridge Presbyterian Church, Fort Lauderdale, FL, Oct. 19, 2003.

CHAPTER 5 — From Civil Wrongs to Civil Rights

1   For a critique of the major studies involving claims of genetic influence, see "Born or Bred? Science Does Not Support the Claim that Homosexuality Is Genetic," Culture & Family Institute, Concerned Women for America, (2004), updated 2009, at: https://concernedwomen.org/born-or-bredscience-does-not-support-the-claim-that-homosexuality-is-genetic/

2   *Bowen* 483 U.S. at 602. See also *Massachusetts Board of Retirement v. Murgia* 427 U.S. 307, 313; *San Antonio Independent School District* 411 U/S. at 28, all cited in Jan LaRue, Esq., "Homosexuals Hijack Civil Rights Bus," Policy

Concerns, Concerned Women for America, 2004, p. 8.

3   *Cleburne* 473 U.S. at 472, cited in LaRue, p. 8.

4   Shawn Zeller, "Marching On, but Apart," *The National Journal*, January 12, 2002.

5   Robert Oliver, "Gay 'Rights' not Analogous to Minority Civil Rights," *Illinois Leader.com*, March 8, 2004, cited in LaRue.

6   Matt Miller, "Here's Every Person and Business Boycotting North Carolina for Its LGBT Discrimination," Esquire, April 13, 2016, at: https://www.esquire.com/news-politics/news/a43931/north-carolina-anti-lgbt-law-boycott/

7   Colleen Jenkins, Daniel Trotta, "Seeking end to boycott, North Carolina rescinds transgender bathroom law," Reuters, March 30, 2017, at: https://www.reuters.com/article/us-north-carolina-lgbt/seeking-end-to-boycott-north-carolina-rescinds-transgender-bathroom-law-idUSKBN1711V4

8   This was spoken to the author of this book and others at a forum on homosexual rights and religious liberties in the late 1990s in Washington, D.C. sponsored by the Ethics and Public Policy Center. Ms. Feldblum defended Tufts University officials for throwing a Christian club off campus over its rule that club leaders had to be Christians who believe God has reserved sexual relations for married couples consisting of one man and one woman. In a biography of Feldblum posted in the "Who Runs Gov" section, the *Washington Post* quoted Feldblum as stating in regard to conflicts between religious freedom vs. gay rights, "I'm having a hard time coming up with any case in which religious liberty should win." https://www.washingtonpost.com/politics/chai-r-feldblum/gIQAywUjAP_print.html.

9   Frederic Bastiat, *The Law*, first published as a pamphlet in 1850, at: http://bastiat.org/en/the_law.html

10 Thomas Jefferson, the Kentucky Resolutions, cited in "The two enemies of the people are criminals and government . . . (Spurious Quotation)," Thomas Jefferson Foundation, at: https://www.monticello.org/site/jefferson/two-enemies-people-are-criminals-and-governmentspurious-quotation

11 Ayn Rand, "Man's Rights," in *The Virtue of Selfishness* (New York: Signet, 1964), p. 111.

12 Introduction, "The Truth about Jim Crow," American Civil Rights Union, 2014, at: http://www.theacru.org/jimcrow/

13 Charles Warren, *The Supreme Court in United States History* (Boston: Little, Brown, and Company, 1922-1924), 3 vols., pp 470-471, cited in Edwin Meese, et al, *The Heritage Guide to the Constitution*, p. 5.

14 Ibid.

15 *Dred Scott v. Sandford* 60 U.S. (19 How.) 393 (1857).

16 *Plessy v. Ferguson* 163 U.S. 537 (1896).

17 Brown v. Board of Education of Topeka 347 U.S. 483 (1954).
18 Meese, "The Meaning of the Constitution," in *The Heritage Guide*, p. 5.
19 In *Engel v. Vitale* 370 U.S. 421 (1962) and *Abington School District v. Schempp* 374 U.S. 203 (1963), the Supreme Court declared school-sponsored prayer and Bible readings unconstitutional.
20 *Roe v. Wade* 410 U.S. 113 (1973), *Doe v. Bolton* 410 U.S. 113 (1973), *Planned Parenthood of Southeastern Pennsylvania v. Casey* 505 U.S. 833 (1992).
21 *Kelo v. City of New London (Conn.)* 545 U.S. 469 (2005).
22 *Romer v. Evans* 517 U.S. 620 (1996).
23 *Obergefell v. Hodges* No. 14–556 U.S. (2015).
24 Ibid, Scalia, J., dissenting, at: https://www.supremecourt.gov/opinions/14pdf/14-556_3204.pdf

CHAPTER 6 — From Redistribution to Economic Liberty

1 Joseph Sobran, *Anything Called a "Program" is Unconstitutional: Confessions of a Reactionary Utopian* (Vienna, Virginia: Griffin Communications, 2001).
2 James Piereson, "The Forgotten Man by Amity Shlaes," book review, *Commentary* magazine, September 1, 2007, at: https://www.commentarymagazine.com/articles/the-forgotten-man-by-amity-shlaes/
3 Ibid.
4 "Trends in Pre-Marital Child-Bearing, 1930 to 1994," U.S. Department of the Census, at: https://www.census.gov/prod/99pubs/p23-197.pdf
5 "Births: Final Data for 2015, National Vital Statistics Reports," Centers for Disease Control, Vol. 66, No. 1, January 5, 2017, at: https://www.cdc.gov/nchs/data/nvsr/nvsr66/nvsr66_01.pdf
6 See, for instance, Patrick Fagan, "The Real Root Causes of Violent Crime: The Breakdown of Marriage, Family and Community," Heritage Foundation report, March 17, 1995, at: https://www.heritage.org/crime-and-justice/report/the-real-root-causes-violent-crime-the-breakdown-marriage-family-and
7 "Confronting the Unsustainable Growth of Welfare Entitlements: Principles of Reform and the Next Steps," Heritage Backgrounder, June 24, 2010, The Heritage Foundation, p. 1, at: https://www.heritage.org/welfare/report/confronting-the-unsustainable-growth-welfare-entitlements-principles-reform-and-the
8 Ibid.
9 Ibid.
10 Heritage report cited in "Block Grants Were THE Key to the Success of Welfare

Reform," the Carleson Center for Welfare Reform, at: http://www.theccwr.org/pdfs/block-grants-were-the-key.pdf

11 "Work Requirements Restored for TANF," Administration for Children & Families, Department of Health and Human Services, August 30, 2012, at: https://www.acf.hhs.gov/media/press/tanf-work-requirements-restored

12 Robert Rector, Vijay Menon, "Obama Gutted Work Requirements for Welfare. Why Trump Is Right to Restore Them," the Daily Signal, August 31, 2017, at: http://dailysignal.com/2017/08/31/obama-gutted-work-requirements-welfare-trump-right-restore/

13 Ibid.

14 Rector, Menon.

15 Blackwell, Klukowski, p. 340.

16 Ibid, pp. 343-344.

CHAPTER 7 — Taxation with Representation

1 Frederic Bastiat, *The Law*, first published as a pamphlet in 1850, at: http://bastiat.org/en/the_law.html

2 P.J. O'Rourke, *Parliament of Whores* (New York: Grove Press, 1991), p. 100.

3 Eugene Volokh, "Government Is Not Reason, It Is Not Eloquence — It Is Force," the Volokh Conspiracy blog, April 14, 2010, at: http://www.volokh.com/2010/04/14/government-is-not-reason-it-is-not-eloquence-it-is-force/

4 James Otis, American Politician, Encyclopedia Britannica, at: https://www.britannica.com/biography/James-Otis

5 Karen Gushta, *How Can America Survive? The Coming Economic Earthquake*, (Fort Lauderdale: Truth in Action Ministries, 2012), p. 156.

6 M.J. Stephey, "The Times Square Debt Clock," *Time* magazine, October 14, 2008, at: http://content.time.com/time/business/article/0,8599,1850269,00.html

7 Robert Knight, "Why Government Must Be Tamed," *The Washington Times*, February 4, 2018, at: https://www.washingtontimes.com/news/2018/feb/4/a-careful-close-look-at-the-debt-clock-shows-a-diz/

8 Tom Paine, "The Rights of Man," cited in John Armor, *These Are the Times That Try Men's Souls: America – Then and Now in the Words of Tom Paine*, (Washington, D.C.: The American Civil Rights Union, 2010), p. 19.

9 Victor Davis Hanson, from *Saving the Republic: The Fate of Freedom in the Age of the Administration State*, edited by Roger Kimball (New York: Encounter Books, 2018, cited in John R. Coyne, Jr. "Defending What Is Best for America," *The Washington Times*, February 13, 2018, p. B-2.

10 Gushta, p. 114.

11 Adam Shaw, "Post-bankruptcy California city tests 'universal' income for residents," Fox News, February 7, 2018, at: http://www.foxnews.com/politics/2018/02/07/post-bankruptcy-california-city-tests-universal-income-for-residents.html

12 Ibid.

13 See: https://economicsecurityproject.org/

14 Ibid.

15 Lee Duigon, "Wrecking Civilization Piece by Piece," *News with Views*, February 8, 2018, at: https://newswithviews.com/wrecking-civilization-piece-by-piece/

16 D. James Kennedy, quoted in Gushta, p. 202.

17 D. James Kennedy, *The Gates of Hell Shall Not Prevail*, (Fort Lauderdale: Coral Ridge Ministries, 1996), p. 233.

18 Bastiat, *The Law*.

CHAPTER 8 — Restoring a Constitutional Form of Government

1 D. James Kennedy, et al., *Reclaiming the Lost Legacy*, (Fort Lauderdale: D. James Kennedy Ministries, 2016), p. 121.

2 Nancy Pelosi, interview, at: https://www.youtube.com/watch?v=08uk99L8oqQ

3 Bishop Robert Barron, "George Weigel's Lessons in Hope," *WordonFire.org*, Sept. 26, 2017, at: https://www.wordonfire.org/resources/article/george-weigels-lessons-in-hope/5594/

4 Stoyan Zeimov, "Super Bowl: Eagles Coach Praises Jesus, Nick Foles Gives Glory to God," *The Christian Post*, Feb. 4, 2018, at: https://www.christianpost.com/news/super-bowl-eagles-coach-praises-jesus-nick-foles-gives-glory-to-god-216348/

5 D. James Kennedy, *The Gates of Hell Shall Not Prevail*, (Nashville: Thomas Nelson Publishers, 1996), p. 234.

6 Ken Klukowski, "Trump Highlights Constitution in SOTU: Judges, Religion, Guns, Terrorists," *Breitbart.com*, January 31, 2018, at: http://www.breitbart.com/big-government/2018/01/31/trump-highlights-constitution-in-sotu-judges-religion-guns-terrorists/